Solo Success

SOLO SUCCESS

100 Tips for Becoming a $100,000-a-Year Freelancer

David Perlstein

THREE RIVERS PRESS *New York*

Published by Three Rivers Press, a division of Crown Publishers, Inc.,
201 East 50th Street, New York, New York 10022.
Member of the Crown Publishing Group.
Random House, Inc. New York, Toronto, London, Sydney, Auckland

www.randomhouse.com

Printed in the United States of America
Design by Susan Hood

Library of Congress Cataloging-in-Publication Data
Perlstein, David.
Solo success : 100 tips for becoming a $100,000-a-year freelancer /
by David Perlstein. — 1st ed.
1. Self-employed. 2. New business enterprises—Management.
I. Title
HD8036.P47 1998
658'.041—dc21 97-44337
CIP

ISBN 0-609-80156-2

10 9 8 7 6 5 4 3 2 1

First Edition

For my loving wife, Carolyn,
who has always stood by me, encouraged me, and
helped to make possible whatever success I've achieved.

ACKNOWLEDGMENTS

I want to thank Dakila Divina, my original editor at Crown Publishers, for responding so positively to my unagented proposal. His commitment to *Solo Success* proves that a good idea *can* make it into print. I am also grateful to Kristin Kiser, who took over for Dakila after he left Crown. Her enthusiasm helped maintain my own during the long process between acceptance of the manuscript and publication.

John Branch, CPA, offered valuable assistance with questions regarding accounting and bookkeeping. I am also thankful to the people I've worked with over the years. I owe much to Ron Spana, who took me under his wing at Jenkins & Ogilvie Advertising in San Antonio; Martin Michael at Michael-Sellers Advertising in San Francisco; and John Fabian, a client, associate, and friend at Fabian and Partners in San Francisco.

I must also express my gratitude to hundreds of clients, past and present. Without their trust in my abilities, I could never have achieved the success that I have enjoyed or written this book.

And finally, I thank my parents, Morris and Blanche Perlstein. The values they taught me by both precept and example have long guided every aspect of my life. May this book be a blessing to my father's memory and a joy to my mother.

CONTENTS

Solo Success

Introduction

GOOD-BYE MR. DITHERS, HELLO MR. DITHERS

It happens several times a year without fail. Someone—often in advertising or marketing—asks me what I do for a living. My response, "I'm a freelance copywriter," elicits an arched eyebrow, a bemused smile, and the comment, "Can you make a living doing that?"

Maybe you're already a freelance copywriter, art director, designer, or marketing consultant. Or perhaps you're a freelance architect, bookkeeper, corporate art consultant, event and party planner, graphic designer, insurance agent, interior designer, investment manager, manufacturers' representative, paralegal or legal secretary, portrait photographer, property management consultant, real estate agent, software programmer, space planner, sign painter, talent agent, or technology consultant. Or maybe you're an employee who has been kicked in the rear once too often in a working relationship requiring you to play Dagwood to someone's Mr. (or Ms.) Dithers—or who fears losing your job altogether as corporate America continues its fascination with downsizing. You're seriously wondering what your own name would look like on letterhead, making *you* Mr. or Ms. Dithers.

Either way, you *can* make a living as a freelancer. And not just a living (ours is no longer a world in which you can get by just by getting by) but a very handsome income. I know firsthand—even though I never would have believed it could happen. So I've written *Solo Success* to share with you what I've learned.

Of course, talent and determination are not, in themselves, sufficient for you to succeed. No matter how polished and powerful your core skills—writing, designing, programming, analyzing, bringing buyers and sellers together—it takes *business sense* (though not on the M.B.A. level by any means) to be your own boss and not fire yourself in despair. This book gives me the opportunity to share with you some of what I've learned since 1979 about running a freelance business. In fact, it's *totally* about the business side of freelancing. Whatever the state of your core skills, which I won't be discussing, I'm definitely optimistic that you can profit from what you read in *Solo Success.* After all, I've used the same principles in the trenches and enjoyed the considerable rewards they can offer.

Mystery money

To be honest, this is the first time I've revealed to a general audience that I make over $100,000 a year as a freelancer (pushing $200,000 as of this writing). Yes, my wife knows. My accountant knows. The IRS knows, of course. And I've told my mother. She's very proud. But then, she'd be proud if I were making $20,000 a year.

Whether my clients have any idea of the size of my income or the scope of my business, I don't know. After all, they pay reasonable fees for my work writing direct mail, brochures, ads, marketing reports, newsletters, radio commercials, and the like. Further, they often view themselves as my only client since they can always count on me to respond quickly to their requests and meet even the tightest deadlines—some of which, by their own admission, are absurd. Most likely my individual clients have no clear concept of how broad my client base usually is, how hard I often have to work to deliver a high level of service, and how rewarding freelancing can be. But then, most people don't really understand what freelancers do. Certainly I didn't when I began.

A providential train ride

I started my career in advertising in 1971—as an employee. Actually, I eschew the word "career." I much prefer to say that I "make a living." I consider a business career, with its ladder of escalating promotions and responsibilities, to be dependent on an employer or series of employers. Since 1979 I have had only clients and nowhere to go in my business hierarchy beyond giving myself grandiose, and meaningless, titles.

That I got into advertising was basically a fluke, considering that my life had been directionless. I grew up in New York City's borough of Queens and attended Alfred University, an outstanding small private school in upstate New York. I majored in English only because I loved to read. I continue to be an avid reader today, even if my focus has shifted from literature to religion, history, and sociology. Having neither career goals nor any interest in graduate school, I enlisted in an army program with guaranteed admission to officer candidate school. Given that this was 1966 and the war in Vietnam was peaking, my family and friends were aghast. I, however, thought that military service would not only help repay the United States for the good fortune my family had enjoyed (I still cannot look at or read about the Statue of Liberty and not tear up) but that it would also provide me with heightened maturity and a sense of direction.

After two months of basic training, two months of advanced infantry training, six months of Infantry Officer Candidate School at Fort Benning, Georgia (which taught me a great many lessons I still cherish and use), and two years as a deputy special services officer at Fort Sam Houston, Texas (highlighted by coaching the post basketball team), I still hadn't a clue about where I was headed. Again a civilian, I was about to be married and was completely perplexed by my role in the world.

I taught English for a year at a private school, thanks to a referral from an insurance agent with whom I had applied for a job—a person kind enough to recognize that I wasn't meant to sell insurance. Following her college graduation, my wife, Carolyn, and I purchased EurailPasses and flew off to London for three months of travel on the cheap. Only by chance did I kill time on a long train ride somewhere on the Continent by reading in *Playboy* an article about advertising by the creative guru turned popular writer (*From Those Wonderful Folks Who Brought You Pearl Harbor*) Jerry Della Femina. Suddenly I saw possibilities for my interest in writing that could be both fun and rewarding.

Chance also led to my first job as a copywriter when we returned to San Antonio in 1971. Unemployed and with time on my hands, I accompanied Carolyn to the alumni employment office at Trinity University. After interviewing Carolyn but finding no openings for her, the counselor asked me if I was looking for a job—a question I had never expected. When I answered affirmatively, she found requests from two small ad agencies, one of which agreed to speak with me. The interview went well, and I began my career in advertising by writing a brochure for Greyhound sight-seeing buses. For the next three years I learned by doing and made my share of mistakes, but also built a small reputation for doing good work.

In 1974, needing a break from the South Texas heat and with Carolyn having been accepted in the graduate program at San Francisco State University, we moved to San Francisco. I had no job waiting for me. After ten weeks of often soul-racking searching, I finally found a job in an agency. While the environment was not as creative as I would have liked it to be, I again had an opportunity to learn many of the lessons that would help me build my own freelance business—lessons not just about advertising but about *the business of running a business,* which can make the difference between success and failure to freelancers in any field.

In 1979 I left—not because the fire to freelance burned hot within me but because I felt that freelancing would give me the time to search for a better job (in advertising, that's a euphemism for building a major TV commercial reel) at a bigger shop. A number of creative directors had nice things to say, but I failed to land an offer.

The first $100,000 is the toughest

Fortunately, the agency I left gave me business. This was only natural since I knew their accounts and creative needs. But the cord was hardly cut. They were responsible for 95 percent of my billings in 1980, my first full year as a freelancer.

Of course, I knew that my income would be reduced at first—not a thrilling prospect considering that Carolyn's career at the time focused on the modest-paying field of creative dramatics and children's theater and that we had a three-year-old son, Seth. However, the rent on our flat was low and we had some money in the bank. I would have been making $33,000 to $35,000 at the agency in 1980, but I figured we could get by on $20,000. Moreover, a freelancer's flexible schedule would give me more time to spend with Seth as well as to write fiction while the sun still shone instead of after work when our household had quieted down.

I have known people who became instantly successful upon making a work or career change, but I was not one of them. My 1980 income was $18,000—barely a living wage in expensive San Francisco and slightly below my projection. Obviously I earned considerably less than I would have on an agency salary with an annual raise. But I believed that I had the talent and determination to keep on. In 1981, still working in our dining room on a desk made from an old hollow-core door and cardboard file cabinets, I raised my earnings to $28,000. My income remained lower than the salary I would have been earning, but it had nonetheless increased substantially. Investing in myself, I bought a new portable typewriter. But then 1982 brought a shock. My income had seemingly peaked, remaining at $28,000, and it still lagged behind what I would have earned as a salaried employee.

But looking at the bright side, I was almost completely weaned from my old agency thanks to a small but growing client base. I was making contacts, getting referrals, and—most importantly—satisfying my clients. In 1983 my income rose to $48,000, so I was drawing about even with, and probably ahead of, what

I might have been making in an agency. And after applying the principles that I've set out in this book—principles learned in the classroom of freelance reality—I celebrated hitting the $100,000 mark in 1986. I was my own boss and ahead of the game in every way. What's more, I had no intention of ever being an employee again.

Downsizing for dollars

Yes, you need luck to succeed as a freelancer. But luck is no more than preparation encountering opportunity. Opportunity tends to knock frequently in life. We're simply not always prepared to recognize it, let alone act on it. *Solo Success* can't open the door to opportunities for you, but it can prepare you to open the door yourself and profit from them. After all, *Solo Success* reflects *proven* success. What I've experienced isn't theory but reality. Naturally, I won't attempt to say that I'm the nation's most successful freelance businessperson. I don't doubt that there are other freelancers right in the Bay Area—in advertising and other fields—whose income is greater than mine. On the other hand, I am sure their number is small precisely because in spite of both talent and experience on the employee level, most people lack the business fundamentals that form the foundation of long-term freelance success. Without a boss or fellow employees to fall back upon, they founder.

What's more, there has never been a better time to freelance than *now.* The restructuring of the American economy has created a great deal of misery, and the media have reported this fact unceasingly. *Fortune* magazine, for example, featuring Scott Adams' Dilbert on its cover, asked *Will You Ever Get Promoted?* and offered a number of "career against the wall" articles such as "6 Ways to Jump-Start Your Career" and "Test for Success: Are You the Most—Or Toast?"

Fortunately the changing American economy has also created highly profitable opportunities for people with the courage to leave the nest and test their wings. Major corporations are operating leaner and meaner to fatten up bottom lines and maintain stock prices. Because freelance help is usually available, small businesses won't risk hiring yet another employee and taking on the additional dollar-devouring overhead that accompanies new staff. In sum, *outsourcing* has become, in the vernacular of contemporary business, a paradigm—one that will remain an important business practice for many years to come.

A word about how to read *Solo Success*

Solo Success isn't a narrative. It's a handbook and guide created to provide advice on whatever issues you may be confronting. For this reason, you may ultimately notice that bits of advice and references to specific tips are repeated in two or more places. This is no accident. While you may wish to read *Solo Success* from first page to last, you can easily skip around if you wish, focusing on the specific chapters and tips that interest you most before moving on to other sections. At the same time, I hope that you will keep this book handy—the equivalent of a friend you can call at any time—since a tip that seems irrelevant today may become critical tomorrow.

Finally, read *Solo Success: 100 Tips for Becoming a $100,000-a-Year Freelancer* with my best wishes. Every story or example is true. Every principle applies across the board, whatever business you're in. And each tip reflects my honest attempt to tell it like it is—including the failings we all must admit to.

When you're finished, I cannot guarantee that you will turn in your resignation without reservations or see your freelance income soar overnight. But I *can* tell you that if you have talent, believe in yourself, take these tips to heart, and stick with them when times are difficult, you can get more out of your career—and your life—than you ever dreamed possible.

To *your* success!

Chapter 1

DISCOVERING MANAGEMENT

Becoming a freelancer bears a resemblance to looking through the opposite end of a telescope. Run your own business, and everything that once seemed familiar suddenly takes on an entirely different perspective. Without question, you find yourself with views about working you may never have had before.

For example, a national advertising agency's San Francisco office once called me in to assist their Chicago office in developing concepts for sales promotion materials. Like much of my work, the project wasn't a high-profile job. Rather, it represented another bread-and-butter task that paid a nice fee and allowed me to play the hero yet again—coming to the rescue when the agency's creative staff was overtaxed and the client's deadline extremely tight. I, of course, would be expected to willingly work nights or Sundays (I don't work on Friday night or Saturday since that is the Jewish Sabbath) if necessary to get the job done on time.

Following a successful review of the initial concepts the creative director and I had developed, the agency manager mentioned how much he loved his work and wondered why his staff was so eager to fly out the door each day at five-thirty. Of course, I knew they often stayed later—that's the nature of the business.

And I knew they undoubtedly resented evening and weekend work. Who could blame them? Employees have lives outside the office. Moreover, when employees see their work week balloon to fifty or sixty hours, they can reasonably be expected to ask, "What's in it for me?" True, they get to keep their jobs, which is no small compensation these days. But their company's profits go to the home office. Senior executives and stockholders grow wealthy while employees settle for a modest holiday bonus.

What makes me, as a freelancer, so willing to work long hours? I don't believe for a second that my love for the craft of copywriting is greater than anyone else's. Nor do I have a more intense personal relationship with the people who hire me than with the members of my family. However, as a freelancer, I get *paid* for *every* job I do. Whenever I'm working, I'm making money. Conversely, if I don't accept the sometimes challenging terms that come with a job, I don't get paid. As a freelancer, *work or else* is a daily fact of life. Given this reality, it's amazing how easily you can tolerate, and even enjoy, the extra hours—and the pressure that goes with being busy—when your rewards parallel your efforts.

However, to make it on your own, you must first undergo a mind shift.

TIP 1

Think like a CEO.

You're top dog in a business enterprise. Run your business with self-confidence and even a bit of attitude.

Become a freelancer, and you enter a new world. You are no longer a writer, designer, agent, programmer, planner, sign painter, or analyst to be hailed for your skills and insight. You are also no longer a teammate to be supported, a staff member to be given assignments, or an employee to be compensated and cared for by the company. You *are* the company.

Before you ever write another word, rough out another layout, call another seller, enter another line of code, determine another schedule, or print out another report, you have to see yourself for what you've become—one more company facing the same challenges and goals embraced by every other business organization in the nation. Once *your* name goes on the letterhead, you have more in common with AT&T and Ted Turner than you ever had with your former fellow employees. You've entered the world of revenue forecasts, budgets, profit and loss statements, and tax planning. In short, even if you still cling to a jeans-and-running-shoes mentality, you must face the fact that part of you has become a *suit.*

Making the transition doesn't require a degree in business. Rather, it requires a high degree of understanding that as a freelancer, you will have to weigh every action you take from the standpoint of *sole personal responsibility.* You alone will make the varied decisions that can build your success.

Welcome the challenge of thinking and acting like a business owner, and you'll provide yourself with an opportunity to achieve what you've always really wanted.

TIP 2

Free yourself from stereotypes.

To some, freelancing suggests being between jobs or not being good enough. Know that as an independent businessperson, you are worthy of respect.

Too often the word "freelancer" carries negative connotations that you must overcome in order to build your business. These connotations involve not only how others see you but *how you see yourself.*

From experience, I know that advertising agency and corporate marketing people often use the term "freelancer" in a pejorative sense. They view anyone who freelances as someone who's out of a job or between jobs. Others think of freelancers as people who were fired for incompetence, who were let go when an account was lost, or who voluntarily set themselves adrift to have a baby, write a screenplay, or get in touch with their inner selves. Tell most people you freelance, and they wonder why you don't have a regular job. After all, they do, and their own insecurities may make them insecure about you.

In reality, the majority of the American workforce—regardless of education, skill level, and even ambition—does not possess an entrepreneurial bent. While freelancing represents the entrepreneurial spirit on a fairly modest level, most people simply are not prepared to struggle with the challenges and uncertainties of being their own bosses. Accordingly, *your* position as a freelancer may strike them as tenuous and temporary at best and threatening at worst. Many people may regard you with a measure of doubt and may express skepticism as to whether you really *can* make a living as a freelancer. Potential clients may doubt your availability over time—even for the duration of a project. This skepticism can weaken not only your position in a relationship (see Tip 5) but your self-esteem as well.

Remind yourself of what you truly are—a company that just happens to have a staff of one. I think of myself as an independent communications company and frequently relate that to clients and prospects. While I am not fond of euphemisms, this choice of words can make a major impact on the way you see yourself and thus on the way clients and prospects see you. After all, you are the chairman of the board and CEO with all the responsibilities and perks that go with those positions. Except for—and often including—the presidents of companies you deal with, your clients will generally be cogs in the wheels of larger organizations. They may work with large staffs and oversee big budgets, but they are still employees. You are not.

Value yourself and your work, and others will raise their opinions to value you as well.

TIP 3

Commit yourself.

Success and effort go hand in hand. Give yourself time and tough your way through the ups and downs that any business faces.

One of the things I miss most about my first years of freelancing is the free time I had to do other things. Of course, I would have been delighted to be working every hour of the day and earning an income to match my efforts. And admittedly, some freelancers who are particularly well connected—either with their former companies or with others they know in their industries—do hit the ground running and keep busy from the moment they distribute their business cards. Most of us, however, need time to get up to speed. Don't let that time become deceiving and even destructive.

Every other day when I get home from my office downtown, I run several miles. On alternate days I lift weights. Working out helps keep my weight down and my spirits up. In those early years of working at home, I was able to run before lunch. We lived half a block from Golden Gate Park, so a jog past eucalyptus trees and around lakes required little more than stepping out of my doorway. After running, I could take a leisurely shower, eat lunch, throw on a pair of shorts on a warm day, and get back to work.

However, I never confused enjoying my free time with thinking that I could achieve success for my growing family (we had our second child, Rachel, in 1981, and our third, Aaron, in 1983) while putting in only a few hours of work each day. Certainly, you can choose a more modest lifestyle and establish income goals and a budget to provide for it (see Tips 21 and 36). If your needs are relatively simple, you can attempt to work just enough to keep the wolf from the door. However, by working on the margins you risk condemning yourself to living on the margins. Clients come and go and relationships end regardless of our best efforts and intentions (see Chapter 10, Tips 81–90 for more on this). Ours is not an age hospitable to businesses that tread water.

Unless you build momentum and go forward, expanding your business and enhancing your cash reserves, you risk falling backward—often rapidly.

Some people certainly do become freelancers to enjoy an idyllic existence. They work casually and keep their distance from the rigors that can overwhelm a business owner. Those who can succeed on this low-key level are certainly worthy of praise and respect. However, most find themselves employees again within a few years, or even a few months—and they are not necessarily happy about it.

So write the great American novel if you have it in you. (I've written five; none have sold.) Paint your heart out. Or build exquisite furniture in your garage or basement. But do it during your carefully allotted personal time. In a highly competitive marketplace, the dream of kicking back and prospering can quickly turn into a nightmare.

To reach the $100,000 level, reach into yourself for the full-time effort such an income requires.

TIP 4

Take off your training wheels.

Prepare yourself to make it on your own by becoming your own support team.

When my children began learning to ride bicycles, they couldn't wait to get rid of those training wheels that reminded them they weren't quite big kids yet. Not surprisingly, however, they were not able to wean themselves from the support that an extra set of wheels offered simply by getting on their bikes. Bicycle riding represents a skill that has to be acquired, and the children gained their confidence a day at a time until they had finally achieved their independence. As a freelancer, you haven't the luxury to work with training wheels. You go it alone from the outset or you don't get going at all. Embrace the challenge, and you will propel yourself a long way toward the success you dream about.

An agency creative director who'd called on my services for many years once asked me to be part of a team to develop a TV commercial for a pizza chain. At our first meeting, both staff and freelance writers met to toss around concepts. After several days we arrived at half a dozen concepts worth putting into script form. One of the freelancers had previously been with a major agency, and there was no question he was very creative. Yet while his concepts gave us real food (pun intended) for thought, they were sketchy, and when the time came to flesh them out, he was unable to submit a finished script. As a result, the creative director asked me to script several of my own concepts (one was later chosen for the sole spot to be produced) and one of my fellow freelancer's concepts as well in order to determine if it was workable. Ultimately, it wasn't.

This freelancer certainly didn't have a problem being a team player. In fact, his biggest problem was being *too* used to group work. As a freelancer he was now expected to carry out his assignment from concept to completion outside of the familiar group setting with no one else to pick up the pieces of his ideas and meld them into a workable whole. In the setting of a large advertising agency, his contributions would have been augmented by others. As a freelancer for whom that kind of team process is rare, he came up short.

The creative director admitted that he'd made a mistake and thanked me for helping cover for the other freelancer. Not surprisingly, that freelancer soon became an agency employee again. A creative director, creative group head, and other writers and art directors could complete what he started, or at least help nurse him toward completion.

As a freelancer, you must stand on your own two feet. You have no boss to guide you, no coworkers to help you when you're stuck, no juniors to hand off a project to with "Let me see something tomorrow afternoon." That's the price of being a one-person company. The evolutionary process that sees you grow into a position of total responsibility is not unlike that of emerging out of adolescence into adulthood. But just as adulthood brings new responsibilities, it also offers new and valuable rewards.

Tackle every job with the understanding that you and you alone are responsible for its success, and your success will follow.

TIP 5

Go eyeball to eyeball.

Let your demeanor demonstrate to your clients that they're dealing with the chairman of the board.

As a freelancer, your goals are fairly simple and straightforward: You want to sell yourself and your work and command fees that are commensurate with your ability. To meet these goals, you must command the respect of your clients. Regardless of their authority over the projects they direct, they must accept you as an equal—and you must see them in the same light.

By approaching a client or prospect hesitantly, feeling uncertain of yourself, you give away a measure of subtle but very real psychological power. A client who sees you as a vendor (see Tip 57 for a discussion of what I call "vendoritis") rather than as a peer can control your relationship in ways that will limit your effectiveness and your income potential. You end up waiting for meetings—an extremely costly process since time spent thumbing through magazines is not as productive as time spent working. You find yourself receiving inadequate background information, which hampers your ability to target the key challenges ahead. Deadlines seem to grow more difficult and demanding. Finally, the client views your work pessimistically and questions both your contribution and your fees, no matter how modest. Worse, you start believing what the client believes—that you're "only" a freelancer (remember Tip 2) and that really talented people work for others. Get real. You're as talented a freelancer as you were an employee!

Without question, the esteem in which you hold your business and yourself will earn you greater client confidence and enable you to discuss your client's business challenges and objectives with greater authority. No matter how large the company, no matter how exalted or powerful the individual client, remember that you have been called in to do a necessary job—one that the people for whom you are working cannot currently perform for themselves. As the senior representative of *your* company, you can meet on equal terms with *anyone* from *their* company.

Carry yourself like the chairman of the board, and you'll carry your business farther, faster.

TIP 6

Flex your independence.

Use your time judiciously to make your workday more pleasant and to ease the burden of your new responsibilities.

By this point—and there are 94 more tips to come—you may be feeling the weight of responsibility bearing down on your shoulders. After all, a freelancer wears many hats—from CEO and chief financial officer to account representative, bookkeeper, and human resources director. And we're not even going to discuss how you can use your core skills more effectively!

Bear in mind, however, that being your own boss and fulfilling multiple roles does offer the kind of flexibility few employees ever enjoy. You can work hard and put in the hours required to meet your clients' needs and still find invigorating time for yourself and your family. Need to go to a parent-teacher conference at your child's school? You can work around it, even rescheduling client meetings when possible. Want to go for a long walk at lunchtime? As long as you can meet your deadlines, you're free to plan your schedule your way. No one has to know—or will care—that you came up with that brilliant idea after the evening news and not at two-thirty in the afternoon. As an employee, your job may greatly depend on *appearing* to be busy and productive. As a freelancer, your business will depend solely on how productive you actually are.

When I can, I leave my office between four and four-thirty so I can run before dinner, and even on non–running days, I'm always home in time to eat with my family. Many employees don't enjoy that luxury on a daily basis. And some simply count on getting home late every night. I freely admit that I may arrive at my office no later than seven-thirty or eight in the morning to compensate for my early quitting time. And I'll definitely bring work home for the evening if I have to. When I agree to meet a deadline, I *meet* that deadline (see Tip 29). But the only standard for scheduling my activities is the one *I* set.

Remember that *you* control your life, and you can keep your life under control while you prosper.

TIP 7

Develop carrots and sticks.

Determine which rewards you'll lavish on yourself for a job well done—while finding reasons to drive yourself to work smarter and more profitably.

Being chairman of the board can be intoxicating at first. And well it should be. No one asks you why you were five minutes late to work or why you didn't come back from lunch sooner. No office politicians wield their sharp tongues behind your back. Promotions—if not pay raises—are yours for the asking. Delightfully, you will never have to suffer a nasty client again—unless you need the business and are compensated sufficiently for any unpleasantness you must endure.

You've got complete control. But you have to *stay in control* to keep your business growing. You have to replace the traditional carrots and sticks—the rewards and fears that inhabit any workplace—with new carrots and sticks of your own.

Some carrots will never have a dollar value. Enjoy your independence and the freedom from organizational hassles that it affords you. When business is good, treat yourself to a small reward like a special dinner or a new article of clothing. When things are slow, use a small portion of your time to do something that lifts your spirits—jogging or a bike ride, a quick visit to a museum exhibit, an afternoon baseball game in the sun, or a quiet walk. While freelancing places big responsibilities in front of you, you are still a human being who cannot be defined by a Form 1040.

Conversely, know when to apply the stick to yourself. When business is good, don't allow yourself to think that you can coast or give anything but your best. Keeping a sense of perspective works two ways. When business is not so good, don't allow yourself to wallow in self-pity or become inert. (In Chapters 8 and 10 we'll discuss some of the things you can do to keep projects coming.)

Develop the right combination of empathy and toughness, and you'll keep yourself on an even keel while you keep your freelance business moving in the right direction.

Chapter 2

DEFINING YOURSELF

The first time I saw New Mexico, I was sitting with the basketball team I coached from Fort Sam Houston. We had ridden for hours from San Antonio to the Fourth Army championships at Sandia Base outside Albuquerque. After we passed through West Texas and Lubbock in the Panhandle, the scenery changed dramatically. The New Mexico horizon, crowned by distant reddish mountains, seemed to extend forever. As a native New Yorker west of the Mississippi for the first time, I had never before encountered such a vista of open space. It presented a truly eye-opening experience.

Running your own business can provide much the same kind of breathtaking awareness that your horizons have expanded dramatically. But that surge of freedom you feel can be misleading. It's wonderful to realize you can be anything you want to be. But it can be quite sobering to realize that unless you determine who you are and what your business is, you can be exposed to unnecessary, and potentially costly, risks.

On the other hand, if you define yourself too narrowly, you may miss profitable opportunities for which you are qualified—even if you have to stretch your talents. Smart freelancers leverage versatility without compromising their strengths.

Knowing what you can and cannot do—indeed, how you should and should not define yourself—requires the famed balance of Sholem Aleichem's Fiddler. You play your tune energetically and joyously, all the while struggling to avoid falling off the roof. Keeping your balance accurately requires only a little thoughtful honesty and the realization that, to paraphrase Mr. Lincoln, you can't please all of the people all of the time.

TIP 8

Avoid conglomeration.

No one can do everything well—or has the time to. Define what you do best, then give it your best.

For over twenty years my professional skills included writing and producing radio commercials. Like other producers, I constantly fielded inquiries from actors, actresses, disc jockeys, and folks who had been told they had a nice voice. All sought fame and fortune in the world of radio and television voice-overs.

Professionals differ markedly from amateurs, but not only in the area of talent. Not surprisingly, most of the very best voice talents throughout the country tend to have a fairly limited vocal and acting or announcing range. (The late Paul Frees, with whom I worked, was one of a fascinating few exceptions. Paul's remarkable vocal range played from Orson Welles to the Pillsbury Doughboy.) But what these voice talents do, they do as well as or better than virtually anyone else.

Amateurs try to impress producers with how *many* voices they can do. They fail not only through lack of talent but also through lack of focus—an inability to find out what they do well and then perfect it. Often they're amazed when a producer hires an actress from Britain rather than an American who attempts to carry off a British accent, or when he casts a seventy-five-year-old actor rather than a thirty-five-year-old who does a caricature of a senior voice.

In much the same way, it's easy for freelancers to fall into the trap of trying to be everything to everybody—particularly with an eye to increasing their status. For example, I have known a number of writers and art directors who have left advertising agencies to set up shop as individual practitioners of specific skills, then announced themselves to be agencies. Being known as freelancers simply didn't offer them enough prestige. However, life as a one-person agency presented them with endless frustrations. Talented people all, these freelancers obviously could not perform all the functions for which clients call on agencies—like strategic planning, media buying, and broadcast production—unless they called on other freelancers. Their new business pitches failed because they couldn't convince prospects that a one-person shop calling in "associates" on a project basis could do a better job than an agency with an established team in place. (Groups of independent associates, on the other hand, can be quite effective. See Chapter 11.) The "virtual company" is a growing reality—but it must be based on truth. Too often the clients a freelancer manages to "fool" prove to be small, troublesome to service, and unprofitable.

To make things worse, functioning ad agencies and design studios that might have called on these freelancers for assistance often shunned them, being wary of hiring a competitor who potentially threatened to contact their clients and take business away.

Expect difficulties when you seek to impress clients as being an organization as opposed to *thinking* like an organization. In today's marketplace, freelancers are excellently suited to performing as many functions for as many kinds of clients in as many situations as present themselves. If you inflate your image, however, you will minimize the opportunity that you as a freelancer uniquely possess—the chance to use your versatility to be what *other* people need *when* they need it in the *way* they need it and to *make money* doing it!

"One" may be a lonely number for dinner, but it is often the perfect complement to ad agencies, design studios, real estate brokerages, corporate marketing and human resource departments, software developers, and other larger entities that know *their* role and depend more frequently than ever on freelancers to help them fulfill it.

TIP 9

Shoot at all the targets.

Know your market. Be realistic about which clients will be interested in your services. And look to small clients for big opportunities.

When I was a kid in New York, a bank robber named Willie Sutton was often on the front page of the local tabloids. His response to the question, "Why do you rob banks?" was often quoted. As Willie tersely explained, "That's where the money is."

Willie knew which doors to knock on within his field of expertise. As a freelancer, you have to do the same. And that can mean rapping your knuckles on doors other than those of Fortune 1000 companies.

Yes, big clients often pay big dollars. If you've already established a heavyweight reputation in your field and not burned any bridges behind you, go at them. But don't overlook smaller clients, who tend to have a greater need for freelance help since their more limited resources often limit their staff. My field, advertising, provides a good example.

Even after all these years, I find it difficult to attract big-agency clients. In fact, I rarely try. Maybe they don't think I'm talented enough. But I believe there's another reason that a formidable big-agency blockade stands in the way of freelancers like me. Big agencies have big clients who demand big staffs to handle their accounts. As a result, big agencies also have big overhead and loads of big expensive egos. Agencies are reluctant to hand out juicy assignments since freelancers' fees generally come out of the bottom line. What's more, big-agency people want to do all the good work themselves—and bask in the glory that accompanies a great TV spot or magazine ad. There's nothing wrong with that. It's just a fact of life.

Smaller agencies, on the other hand, often build their businesses around freelancers. Departments in large corporations also frequently turn smaller assignments over to freelancers when staff members are busy—or simply to keep their paid staffs from growing too large. A little modesty regarding the nature of your clients can bring you a more than modest income. But then, Willie Sutton would have said the same thing.

Be willing to lower your sights and you may raise your income significantly.

TIP 10

Deglamorize.

Glamorous projects are always appealing, but they're not always available at large companies. Leverage small jobs to turn big companies into big clients.

Find the right kind of client (see Tip 9), and you've won half the battle. But I'm not suggesting that you have to limit yourself to small clients. Big clients can prove profitable as well when you determine *which* jobs are available to you.

The field of television commercials offers a perfect example. For many, if not most, freelance copywriters and art directors, the lure of television is as strong as the song of the sirens who nearly beckoned Odysseus to his death on his sea journey homeward to Ithaca from Troy. You may remember that Odysseus had himself tied to the mast to resist the sirens' call and prevent the destruction of his crew.

Advertising has been known as "the show business of business"—the most visible facet of almost any company's operations. Who wouldn't like to work on a major TV spot with a production budget of half a million dollars or more and breakthrough visual effects? And how about getting to work side by side with a well-known film, TV, or sports star in the course of creating a thirty-second epic? Witness the ritual of introducing new commercials during the Super Bowl—an event that has become almost as big as the game itself. These commercials generate talk from industry insiders and the public for months. Those who make them are listened to attentively at cocktail parties for the rest of the year, since TV commercials have also become a medium of mass entertainment.

The problem for freelancers is that ad agencies control almost all sizable TV commercial creation. And since agency people tend to live for TV commercials, they generally do all the work themselves.

Likewise, if you're an event planner, you may find that work on a corporation's international sales meeting never leaves the human resources or training department. If you're an editor, you may discover that all the effort that goes into a blockbuster novel by a famous author stays inside the publisher's office. If you're a legal secretary, you might not find yourself working on the trial of the century when a law firm needs extra help. But that doesn't mean that large companies can't become good clients.

Even if the front door doesn't swing wide open, the back door to a big company may be graced by a great big welcome sign—if you're willing to do the less glamorous jobs. For example, creative people at major ad agencies don't like doing brochures. I love working on brochures because I love getting paid. For the same reason, I've written product labels and sales presentations as well as direct mail copy, ads, and commercials.

Realism, not egotism, builds a profitable freelance business. How can you keep your dreams and your income in balance?

Reflect on the reasons you're in business for and by yourself. You want to dispense with office politics, gain flexibility, and keep 100 percent of the profits you generate. You can sacrifice glamour and still do outstanding work for a good fee.

Remember number one. More humble projects at big companies may not set tongues to wagging in fashionable restaurants and clubs, but they can build a powerful long-term freelance business. In fact, you could end up earning as much as, or more than, the folks who work on glamour projects but pass the profits on to their employers.

Deflate your ego and you can inflate your income.

TIP 11

Cultivate a multiple personality.

Go beyond narrow specialization to develop a variety of strengths that will broaden your business base.

Not long ago, I received a call from a former client who had left his family-owned business a year earlier to go out on his own. He was wondering how to get new clients for his one-person consulting business and took me to lunch to help him develop and refine some ideas. I was delighted to do it since he had been supportive of me for many years. His new status also afforded the potential for a future relationship.

One of his biggest problems was deciding how to present himself. On the one hand, he had a considerable background in a particular industry. On the other, he also had expertise in marketing, the function he had performed for the company he had left. Should he promote his industry expertise or his marketing experience?

My answer was simple: promote both.

The key, I offered, was to treat each strength as a separate facet of his business. Although a freelancer ("consultant" sounds more impressive, but he realized that freelancing was just what he was doing), he was actually chairman of the board of a going concern. To maximize his opportunities, he would need one CEO to run his industry-oriented business and a second CEO to run his marketing-oriented business. Of course, he would have to wear both of those hats as well.

His face lit up. What had been a perplexing problem suddenly became an intriguing challenge. He would have to reach two different markets by developing two sets of communications tools. Fortunately, these could be kept simple. Importantly, they would be effective because each would be highly targeted.

As a freelancer, you may be able to do a variety of projects for a number of different types of clients. The trick to doing so? Make sure you understand every job you seek. If you're in advertising and you're a great TV writer, you can also become a great brochure writer—as long as you understand the principles of writing without moving images and sound as well as the need to extend a message beyond thirty seconds. If you're an art director with multiple awards for print ads, you can also become a talented direct mail professional—as long as you understand that the only common thread between DM and ads is ink printed on paper. If you're an event planner who knows how to bring two hundred salespeople together at a resort, you can also stage wonderful wedding receptions—as long as you understand the difference between a hospitality suite and a honeymoon suite. If you're an information systems manager who can implement comprehensive financial software across an enterprise, you can also enlighten small business accounting staffs on the intricacies of off-the-shelf software—as long as you understand that a client's bottom line leads right to your own.

You can specialize, of course. But the more tasks you can perform, the more broadly you can build your client base. Develop a multiple personality based on knowledge of each medium you can claim as your own, and you'll develop multiple opportunities to grow and prosper.

Chapter 3

GETTING STARTED

Silicon Valley is right down the road (Highways 101 and 280, specifically) from San Francisco. So, like most freelancers in the Bay Area, I do a lot of work for technology companies. Most are "long-established"—in business five years or more, that is. Some, however, are start-ups utilizing their first round of venture capital.

The huge quantity of dollars flowing into start-ups is particularly intriguing considering that Bill Hewlett and David Packard (Hewlett-Packard is a valued client of mine) started one of the world's most dynamic companies in a garage. But while luring bright, talented people and conducting research and development takes a great deal of money in today's economy, getting started as a freelancer can be achieved with very modest funds. The real key to success is your investment in planning and resources, matched by a willingness to stay with it over the long haul.

My own freelancing adventure began with a total cash outlay of less than $900. That bought me such items as basic legal and accounting advice, a fictitious name filing (new businesses in San Francisco must file a notice stating the owner's name and address), letterhead and business cards (printed in one color—black), a small quantity of office supplies, and a second telephone line and phone for my home. I already had a desk—a hollow-core door atop two cardboard file cabinets in our dining room—and a typewriter. Renting office space was out of the question, and anyway, I wanted to be available to take care of our then only child, Seth, who was three.

Can the prospect of going into business for yourself seem daunting? Certainly. It *is* a major step. So don't worry if you sometimes worry. That's also part of the price you pay to become an independent businessperson. But remember, too, that there isn't an employee in the nation who doesn't worry about raises, promotions, competition, office politics, and whether or not there will be a job waiting the next day and the day after that. As a freelancer, you're merely exchanging one set of concerns for another.

Once you get your thinking straight (see Chapters 1 and 2), begin to plan how you'll conduct your business *before* you hang out your shingle—or create your Web site. With the fundamentals in place, you'll provide yourself with the support you need to do business effectively and efficiently. And that's what builds success.

TIP 12

Orient your compass.

Write a business plan to set your basic goals, analyze approaches to achieving them, and stay disciplined as you move your business forward.

Businesses and vacations often have a lot in common. With both, you may know where you want to go and what you want to do, but you can't reach your destination without a certain amount of planning. The last time we went to Hawaii, for example, we decided to stay at Waikiki, since Carolyn had long dreamed of vacationing there and wanted to visit Oahu's cultural centers. But a family of five doesn't get far without paying attention to detail—the budget for the trip, the right time (school vacation), sufficient accommodations (two reasonably priced one-bedroom condos looking out at Diamond Head), and flight schedules that brought four of us out from San Francisco and our oldest from San Diego through Los Angeles.

Of course, once we got to Waikiki, we were free to do as we pleased. My favorite outing was an early morning climb up Diamond Head from the inside of the crater to look out over the Pacific and a large swatch of Oahu. Having arrived at any vacation destination, you can freelance to your heart's content. In business, however, freelancing and improvising are definitely not synonymous.

It's no accident that CEOs, division managers, and department managers of successful companies all write or contribute to annual business plans. Boards of established corporations and potential investors in start-up companies demand that management have a firm grasp of their company's strengths and weaknesses and a clear set of goals by which to measure progress and success. As chairman and lead investor in your freelance enterprise, you must hold yourself to the same standard.

Having discovered your new management responsibilities (Chapter 1) and begun defining yourself and your business role (Chapter 2), you'll need to take the next step. I recommend that you read the rest of *Solo Success,* then write your business plan before you do anything else. Why commit your plan to writing? No matter how much you've gone over your freelance business in your mind or chatted with family and friends, writing provides the discipline necessary to fully develop your thoughts. You'll be amazed at how your perceptions may change—and solidify—once you transfer your thoughts to your computer, word processor, or pad.

In separate sections, commit to words the direction you will take with each of the following:

Core skills. Analyze the strengths that will determine the types of projects you should be seeking and the weaknesses you can overcome to build new skills and opportunities.

Business skills. Ascertain which business skills you need to improve and what specific actions you can take to improve them. Books and magazines, college classes, workshops and seminars, and professional consultations all offer opportunities to develop or polish skills.

Client base. Determine the sorts of clients you can initially target based on your core skills, experience, and contacts, and decide how you will attract them. Project which kinds of clients—by type, size, and location—offer you the most attractive long-term opportunities for growth. Then set objectives for how many of these clients you will add to your roster and over what time periods. (For a detailed discussion of winning new business, see Chapter 9.)

Office and equipment. Determine where your office will be now, and decide on the best location and description of your office five years from now. List your minimal equipment requirements for start-up and what equipment you will want to own or lease over the next five years as your business grows. (See Tips 14, 35, and 36 for discussions of basic business equipment, office supplies, and budget control.)

Financial goals. Assess how much income you can reasonably expect in your first six months and first year, then project anticipated income over the next five years. (See Tip 34 for details on setting goals.)

Just as sports coaches prepare for game after game, season after season, you'll want to write a business plan annually after analyzing your past year's performance (see Tip 39). You needn't be as rigidly detailed as the Silicon Valley CEO for whom I once wrote speeches—his *life* was planned out year after year. The short- and long-term goals expressed in each new business plan may vary considerably from one year to the next due to changes in the general economy, the industry or industries with which you're involved, and your personal needs and desires. But set a carefully considered course for your business, and you'll point the way to success while other freelancers—despite their talent—fall by the wayside in confusion.

TIP 13

Adopt fiscal schizophrenia.

Maintain separate business and family checking accounts to avoid confusion and foster better record keeping.

If you've ever gone out to dinner with friends and then tried to divide the bill fairly, you already understand the reason for this tip. If you and your friends mingle funds together at the table, confusion reigns. After coffee, you can spend fifteen or twenty minutes just trying to figure out who had the large salad and who the half-order, who didn't order an entrée, and how to apportion the tip and tax.

Without question—and without fail—set up a separate business checking account and use it *only* for your business to:

Maintain a sufficient balance to cover business expenses. It's difficult, if not impossible, to know if you have enough money for your business expenses when you're writing checks on a single account to cover mortgage payments or apartment rent, groceries, car insurance, a new pair of jeans, and pocket cash.

Maintain a sufficient balance to cover household expenses. You need to meet your household obligations, a task that can be challenging if you're paying business expenses out of the same account.

Track your business income. If you live in a two-income household, you'll need to figure out whose deposits are whose. If you both freelance, this can be difficult. Your business check register should record *only* business income. What's more, be sure to record the date the check was deposited, the client it was from, and the check number. Banks do lose checks on occasion. Just as unfortunate, client checks can fail to clear due to insufficient funds.

Verify your business expenses. It's time-consuming to go through your personal checks in order to identify or verify business expenses. It's easy to make mistakes, too. And an expense not filed on your income tax returns costs you money needlessly.

To think like a businessperson, you have to *act* like a businessperson (see Tip 1). Most companies maintain *multiple* accounts, each dedicated to a different function, to help simplify their money management.

Your business checking account represents your commitment to the business of freelancing. Split your checking functions to keep your finances together.

TIP 14

Run the numbers.

Freelancing can be a shoestring operation, but even shoestrings cost money. Set a budget for the services and supplies you'll need.

Shortly after I left the advertising agency I'd worked for in San Francisco, an account executive there decided to open an agency of his own. His former boss, who was selling his business to a national agency, saw no problem with that and was quite willing to provide guidance whenever asked. The AE, however, was a man who gloried in office politics. Over the years, he had undermined virtually all of his coworkers and, in doing so, hurt the agency as well. Not surprisingly, he was universally disliked. Also not surprisingly, the president of the agency, lacking his staff's up close and personal point of view, thought well of him. Or at least he did until the AE took samples of all of the agency's forms—from job organizers to purchase orders to invoices—in order to create forms and an agency business structure of his own. His attempt to save money cost him dearly as the relationship with his former boss soured. He could have had the forms just by asking. Moreover, he needlessly lost an excellent source of advice and support.

As a freelancer, you will have to make an investment in your business. Fortunately, that investment can be modest. But most freelancers soon realize that every dollar can be precious. To make the most of the money you've put aside—or should put aside—create a detailed budget. The following budgets—start-up and monthly—contain many of the core services and items you may need to do business professionally right from day one.

Sample Start-up Budget

PROFESSIONAL FEES		
☐ Attorney	$________	
☐ Accountant fees	________	
☐ Fictitious name, business registration	________	
☐ Local business license or tax	________	
☐ Trade publication subscriptions	________	$________

BUSINESS SERVICES		
☐ Initial bank checks		$________

COMMERCIAL OFFICE RENT		
☐ Security deposit	$________	
☐ First and last months' rent	________	
☐ Related equipment rental	________	$________

OFFICE EQUIPMENT		
☐ Desk	$________	
☐ Chair	________	
☐ File cabinet	________	
☐ Computer or word processor	________	
☐ Software	________	
☐ Printer	________	
☐ Modem	________	
☐ New telephone line	________	
☐ Telephone and answering machine	________	

☐ Fax machine	________	
☐ Photocopier	________	$________

BUSINESS CARDS AND LETTERHEAD		
☐ Design	$________	
☐ Printing	________	$________
OFFICE SUPPLIES		
☐ Paper	$________	
☐ File folders	________	
☐ Large (9- by 12-inch) envelopes	________	
☐ Notebook	________	
☐ Pen, pencils, paper clips, etc.	________	
☐ Calculator	________	$________
TOTAL		$________

Monthly Budget

☐ Office rent	$________	
☐ Equipment (computer, furniture) lease	________	
☐ Telephone	________	
☐ Voice mail or answering service	________	
☐ E-mail access	________	
☐ Bank service charge	________	
☐ Postage and stamps	________	
☐ Office supplies	________	
☐ Parking and transportation	________	
☐ Messenger services and overnight shipping	________	
☐ Advertising (e.g., Yellow Pages)	________	
☐ Subscriptions	________	
☐ Bookkeeper	________	
TOTAL		$________

Depending on what your freelance specialty is, you may have additional expenses such as photo and image CDs, a good cassette recorder, a VCR, or specialty reference books and CDs.

Chances are, opening your own business won't cost you a fortune. If you're going to work at home, you may already have a desk—or a table that will function as one—as well as a computer and peripherals. If you don't have teenage children, you can get away with using your home phone as your business phone and take messages as you do now. If you're good about keeping your checkbook up to date and balanced, you can probably keep your own books (I do), with some guidance from your accountant (a must).

However much—or little—you'll have to spend to get up to speed, determine what you will have to invest in your start-up and where you can prioritize to defer expenses until your cash flow and income begin to provide extra dollars. Take control from the beginning, and you'll begin well.

TIP 15

Seek professional help.

A delightfully simple business can become very complex. See an attorney and an accountant first.

If you examine the back pages of community and neighborhood newspapers, you'll often find weekly listings of new businesses, their owners' names, and the legal names by which the businesses will be known. Local and state laws often require the filing of a business name, even if the business name and your own are the same and you're not incorporated. I had no idea about fictitious names, federal ID numbers, business licenses, and Internal Revenue requirements when I decided to freelance. But I did know an attorney who specialized in small business affairs, and he referred me to an accountant whose successor still works with me.

Contact an attorney *before* you take on your first freelance job. If you're already freelancing, seek legal advice to make sure you haven't compromised yourself. When you set up your appointment, find out how much you will be charged. Then go into the meeting with a prepared list of questions to save time and keep focused. You may wish to ask about these details:

- The requirements for establishing a business identity
- The structure of your business identity—sole proprietorship or corporation
- The process for completing required paperwork and filing fees
- Potential liability and protection

Ask your accountant about

- Basic bookkeeping requirements
- Sales tax obligations
- Home office deductions
- Work-related travel expenses
- Depreciating versus expensing major equipment purchases
- Tracking automobile expenses
- Medical insurance premium deductions, which now offer freelancers a major tax break
- Filing quarterly estimated taxes (see Tip 20)
- Filing Form 1099 for unincorporated subcontractors (see Tip 95)
- Guidelines for a tax-deductible retirement plan with tax-deferred interest (see Tip 38)

Further, if you feel that keeping track of client payments and business expenses is more than you can handle, ask your accountant for a bookkeeping reference. Many freelance bookkeepers work for small clients, often as little as two or three hours a month. Your accountant can tell you how to make that arrangement work.

When it comes to laws and taxes—both of which are complex and continually changing—shooting from the hip can blow a major hole in your business. Get your business running smoothly by seeking professional advice at the outset.

TIP 16

Leverage your name.

Your good name can be one of your best business assets. Keep your name in the name of your business.

In 1983, four years after I went freelance, I decided to compartmentalize myself and open a radio commercial production company. Actually there was nothing new about that business entity. As previously, I contacted clients, wrote scripts, cast talent, and then produced and directed the session. I felt, however, that I might do better if the company had its own name and seemed to be a separate entity larger than that of a freelance business.

I called the company American EarLines, registered my fictitious name statement, developed a theme—"radio commercials that really fly"—and had an illustrator friend design a logo with a cute rounded airplane wearing headphones. Over the next six or seven years, I created hundreds of radio spots, mostly local and regional.

I was reasonably happy with the success of American EarLines. But because I was doing so much other work—print, direct mail, and collateral—as David Perlstein, freelance writer, I never grew American EarLines into a full-time occupation. And along the way I discovered that my two identities might actually be costing me business. Freelance clients had no idea that I worked in radio. Because I tended to separate the two entities, any exposure to American EarLines would not connect to me. Radio clients, on the other hand, often had diverse needs but didn't realize that I worked in other media. Furthermore, I couldn't comfortably ask them about print and direct mail since I was a radio commercial producer by definition.

Ultimately, I let my American EarLines identity fade away, along with the separate set of books I kept. And once I decided to concentrate all my efforts on being David Perlstein, my life became easier.

This story has a simple point. Over time, you've made contacts wherever you've worked—coworkers, clients, service providers whom you've hired or worked with, and fellow freelancers—and all of these people know your name. Make the most of that recognition.

Over the last few years a number of advertising agencies—including some hot creative shops—have eschewed using their partners' individual names or their corporate parents' names in favor of impersonal identities. San Francisco, for example, is home to agencies like Black Rocket and Highway One. This may work for an organization whose principals are well connected, but it can limit a freelancer's much-needed exposure.

Throughout my freelance career, I've been amazed by the number of people who have come to know—or know of—me. I attribute that as much to my long tenure in the business as to my creative skills. Either way, my name has worked for me both when former clients and contacts have retrieved it from their Rolodexes years after we met, and when I've received referrals from people who knew people who knew me—referrals whose original sources I often can't even trace.

Put *your name* on your door, business card, and letterhead, and you'll provide the kind of recognition that opens doors to unexpected—and profitable—new contacts.

TIP 17

Create an image.

Develop a business card and letterhead that express your personality and communicate your work style.

In 1988 I left my home office to work in an office at the edge of downtown San Francisco. The location, on Broadway, was both convenient and colorful. The city's remaining topless joints were two blocks away. So were Chinatown, North Beach, the Financial District, and the Embarcadero, which was once the site of a major shipping industry and has since become home to a number of nationally recognized ad agencies and design firms.

Naturally, I needed a new business card and letterhead, and I was not fond of the bland approach I had taken before. I wanted my new materials to make a statement reflecting my personality and sense of humor. So I added a simple new touch:

FLAMBOYANT
LOGO
GOES HERE

David Perlstein

It worked! That simple box above my name on my business card and letterhead almost always elicits a laugh or chuckle and breaks the ice before a meeting with a prospect or a new client. And, since I'm not a designer, it demonstrates my copywriter's conceptual skills in a copywriter's medium.

In 1993 I moved to a new location a block and half away and again decided that the design was too bland. So I had a designer friend add more graphic pizzazz with a three-color treatment. My business card went to eye-opening yellow with red and black accents. Of course, the line "Flamboyant Logo Goes Here" remained. It still produces the same positive reaction every time, even from people in staid corporate environments—or perhaps, *especially* from those people.

Business cards and letterhead are simple items. And no card, letterhead, or envelope will persuade anyone to use your services. But the first impression you make is critical, and a good first impression can set the tone for a lasting relationship.

Whatever budget you have available (creativity doesn't have to be expensive), put your personality out front. Use what makes you a unique individual to make a unique and memorable impression on clients. Your self-confidence will translate into client confidence in you.

TIP 18

Become a control freak.

Set up client and job files, along with a daily job schedule, to stay on top of every task.

No one is born totally organized. One look at any of my children's rooms (ages twenty, fifteen, and thirteen as I write), and that supposition becomes highly evident. I must confess that I too had a lot to learn before I was able to keep track of multiple tasks and meet their individual deadlines.

The army helped. At Infantry Officer Candidate School at Fort Benning, Georgia, each of us had to place every piece of uniform clothing and every personal article in our footlocker or closet in a predetermined place—in a predetermined way. That included folding socks and rolling T-shirts in a rigidly prescribed manner.

I learned another valuable lesson soon after I started work in San Francisco, although I'd already been in the agency business for three years. Naturally, I wanted to maintain a written record of each job I was doing, and there were always several jobs open at any one time. My "solution" was to note the due date of each job on my desk calendar. Not good.

Part of the problem was that if a certain job was due on March 20, my only visual record of that job would pop up on March 20, which allowed little time to actually do the job if I'd neglected to browse my calendar earlier. Another part of my problem was that the agency president came into my office one day and asked me what jobs I was working on and how I'd organized them. I started flipping through my calendar. He flipped. And for good reason!

When I started my freelance business, I was prepared. You can create your own system for keeping track of your projects, if you wish, or you may wish to base it on mine, which includes two key sets of documents.

Permanent job assignment record. I keep this record in my computer (I also keep the billing portion of this information in my ledger so that I have a fail-safe backup system), and I maintain one file for each year. It looks something like this:

1997 Job Assignments

Date	*No.*	*Client*	*Job Description*	*Due*	*Done*	*Fee*	*Billed*	*Paid*	*Amount*	*Balance*
1–3	3843	Redd	*Time* Mailing	1–19	1–19	2,500	1–22	2–20	2,500	0
1–6	3844	Greene	Trade Mag. Ad	1–12	1–11	1,000	1–20	2–19	1,000	0
1–7	3845	Brown (Lou)	"Power" Bro. 97-102	2–3	___	1,500	___	___	___	___

To maintain your records accurately, assign a number (you can also use it as your invoice number) for every job you do, no matter how small. It doesn't matter what kind of numbering system you use as long as it's consistent. I use a simple sequential system; I started with 1001 back in 1979. If you like, you can prefix your numbers with the year of origin (97-1, 97-2) and with a client code (RED 97-1, GRE 97-2). Enter each job, including the day it was opened, the due date, the fee, and the billing and payment record. If you have multiple contacts at an agency or client, include the contact's name as well to avoid confusion. And always enter your client's job and/or invoice number as well to facilitate getting paid on time.

Daily schedule. Almost every day I revise and print out a list of jobs, tasks, and phone calls to keep on my desk. It looks something like this:

THURSDAY
May 4

Due	*Done*	
JOBS		
Tue, 5–9	______	Greene trade magazine ad
Thu, 5–11	______	Gray capabilities brochure
Wed, 5–17	______	White accounting software direct mail package
Fri, 5–19	______	Redd newsletter concepts
TASKS		
Fri, 5–5	______	Self-promotion mailer
Mon, 5–8	______	Estimate to Gray for DM package
CALLS		
Fri, 5–5	______	Joan re Gray design bid
Mon, 5–8	______	Dan re time for Greene presentation
Mon, 5–8	______	Accountant re computer lease

Some days your list may be long. Mine has often included a dozen or more jobs in some state of development (concept, first draft, revision). Other days it may be short. Get organized, and you'll always know just what you're working on and how to plan your day accordingly.

TIP 19

Play pack rat.

Maintain a ledger detailing your invoices, income, and expenses. And keep those printed receipts handy.

Face it. You're now getting into the nitty-gritty that separates successful freelancers from those who wonder, "If I'm so talented, how come I'm not making it?" In fact, the more creative most freelancers are, the more most wonder, "If I'm so talented, how come I have to do all this bookkeeping stuff?" And there's the point.

As an employee, your business paperwork may have been minimal or even nonexistent. Your biggest challenge may have been finding your credit card receipt for that lunch with a client two weeks earlier. Your accounting department did the rest. As a freelancer, *you* are the accounting department.

Start by talking with a CPA. Find out all the requirements you'll have to meet to be prepared at tax time. While IRS regulations are complex, bookkeeping for freelancers doesn't have to be. Here are the essentials:

Income. In your ledger or computer (see Tip 19), enter every job you bill. I include five items here. The first is the *total invoice,* which includes my fee plus any out-of-pocket expenses to be rebilled. The second is my *fee* alone. When I track my billings (see Tip 39), I'm really concerned with the fees I've generated. A $1,500 job consisting of a $1,500 fee and no rebillable expenses represents 50 percent more income than a $2,500 job that reflects only a $1,000 fee and $1,500 in rebillable expenses. When you receive payment, enter the *date* as well as the *amount,* and the *balance due,* if any, in separate columns. This will help you determine not only monthly income but whether an invoice is overdue (see Tips 54–58) and what payment pattern a particular client has developed.

Expenses. You need to do two key things here. First, keep a detailed list of all expenses in your ledger or computer. Your accountant can show you how to set up your books, although there's no one necessary method. I organize my expenses according to chronology and category.

□ *Chronology.* I enter each individual expense, including the date and type or purpose, and I do this daily to avoid falling behind. This way I can very quickly identify any expense and its purpose. (This can be handy if a supplier claims not to have been paid or if a check gets lost or stolen.) I also keep a running total so I know how much I've spent for the year and can rapidly calculate my total expenses for each month and quarter as well.

□ *Category.* Essentially I follow the categories in Schedule C of IRS Form 1040. The categories in Schedule C are limited and serve only as guidelines, but you can add special ones of your own. I keep running totals under the following columns:

Advertising
Bank service charges
Business gifts
Contributions
Dues and publications
E-mail access
Legal and professional services
Local taxes
Meals and entertainment
Medical insurance
Messengers and overnight delivery
Office furniture and equipment
Office rent
Office supplies
Repairs and service
Stamps and postage
Taxis, transit, parking, and tolls
Telephone

If you do this, you can accurately determine your monthly and quarterly income and keep your expenses under control throughout the year. When the year is over, you can instantly enter your expenses on the worksheet your accountant provides without having to look through folders or shoe boxes for receipts and then categorize them.

Receipts. The IRS once called me in for a routine audit. As you can imagine, they refused to take my word that everything was in order, even though I'm an honest citizen. They asked to see my ledger, checkbook registers, canceled checks, and expense receipts—and not just for the past year but for several years. Problem? No. I'd kept my records in good order from day one.

Like it or not, you must create and retain files for receipts—one file per year. You'll want to include your appointment calendar to back up travel, entertainment, and related expenses. Remember, you can afford to keep your home a mess with dirty laundry scattered on the bedroom floor and pizza boxes on the living room couch, but you can't expect to go head-to-head with the IRS unless you keep every receipt and record. Talk to your accountant, set up your system, and keep it current *no less than weekly* to avoid falling behind—and falling victim to late filing fees or an IRS audit of your own.

TIP 20

Skim your tax dollars.

You're now responsible for making your own deductions from the checks you receive. Create a tax account and fund it first.

A series of TV commercials for an auto transmission repair chain used to end with a mechanic warning, "You can pay me now, or you can pay me later." The point was clear: don't risk having a small problem become a major—and costly—one. The same logic applies to handling your tax obligations.

As a freelancer, you are required to make quarterly payments to cover federal taxes—as well as state and local taxes where applicable—on all income earned on a contract basis and reflected in Schedule C of your tax return. One-fourth of your anticipated yearly tax obligation, generally based on your previous year's income, must be sent to the IRS and other appropriate agencies on a predetermined quarterly schedule:

- April 15: You pay in advance for the first tax period of the new tax year.
- June 15: Watch out for this one. You have only *two* months, not three, to come up with another quarter's worth of cash.
- September 15: Be careful, because a long summer vacation could cut into your cash flow.
- January 15: You have a bit of a breather since there's no mid-December payment, which would come during the holidays when most people need cash for gifts and entertaining. Here's a good chance to stock up and get a running start on April 15, when the whole process will begin again.

When the quarterly-payment due date falls on a weekend or holiday, it moves to the next business day.

All this may sound intimidating, but it doesn't have to be, as long as you're aware that your clients do *not* make deductions for income tax, Social Security, Medicare, disability, and the like. As long as you work on a contract basis, your clients will pay you the full amount of your invoice. The trap? You may think that a check for $1,000 is all yours. It's not! Every dollar of every fee that's paid to you represents *gross* income from which one or more governments will demand a share.

Your job is (1) to make every quarterly payment on time and for the full amount due, (2) to have extra cash on hand to cover additional taxes on April 15 if your income goes up—taxes on this additional profit will not have been paid during the previous four quarters, and (3) to cover higher quarterly payments based on increased income. Here's how you do it:

Open a separate,* dedicated *savings or money market account. *Don't* put tax funds in any kind of mutual fund or other investment vehicle that can lose value; you could get a nasty shock at tax time. While the interest your tax funds earn may be modest, those funds are for short-term use only. You want them liquid and secure.

Determine the percentage of your* gross *income that goes to all your taxing agencies. Figure this after Schedule C business deductions but before 1040 personal deductions, mortgage interest deductions, and the like. Total taxes paid divided by gross income will give you that figure. Remember that this figure is *not* the same as your tax bracket. Your accountant can help with this.

Deposit each check you receive in your* separate, dedicated *business checking account. Mingling business funds with those in a family account isn't illegal for sole proprietors; it's just foolish. (See Tip 13.)

In your ledger or checkbook, keep a running tab of the amount due from each check for taxes. This covers your fee only, not any out-of-pocket expenses you may have added to your invoice. If taxes represent 30 percent of your gross income, your record might look like this:

Date received	*Check*	*Fee received*	*Tax owed (30%)*	*Payment to tax fund*	*Cumulative taxes owed*
2–19	Greene #10244	1,000.00	300.00	0	300.00
2–20	Gray #002388	2,500.00	750.00	0	1,050.00
2–26	Black #4062	1,500.00	450.00	0	1,500.00
3–1	Payment	____	____	1,500.00	0

Once or twice each month—I do it on the first and the fifteenth—write a check from your business account to your tax account and reduce your balance. If you anticipate growing your business or if you want to force yourself to save additional money for emergencies or other uses, increase your percentage. It's better to put more into your tax account than less since you can use any extra funds that accumulate at some later date.

So what do you do if a client puts you on the payroll to satisfy its own accounting needs and makes deductions from your checks? Keep on deducting yourself, taking sufficient funds out to make sure you meet your percentage and to provide extra funds in your tax account if desired.

By all means, ask your accountant for advice. But remember, the responsibility to provide for tax payments is yours alone. Make your tax payments *first.* Then pay yourself for living expenses, savings, and investment.

TIP 21

Go bare bones.

Base your living expenses on the lowest income you can possibly expect, put your family budget in writing, and then live with it for your first year.

If you have read the Introduction, you know that my income dropped substantially when I started freelancing. It wasn't until my fourth full year that my income caught up to where it would have been had I stayed with the agency. The next year and every year after that it zoomed higher, and I ended up way ahead.

You might do better than I did right from the start, of course. Maybe you'll do much better. An account executive at a former agency client of mine—a bright guy with major agency experience in New York and Chicago as well as San Francisco—finally became fed up with his job and formed an agency of his own. Working out of his garage, he found some small clients and brought in his wife to provide art direction. A year later he had major accounts, an office suite, and a staff. I remember going to see him at his office and waiting while he finished a meeting with his accountant so that he and his wife could decide what to do with all the money they'd just made.

You'll be better off, however, if you expect your income to drop during your initial year—or years. What to do? First, consider any money you're giving up as an investment, not an expense. Chances are, you'll need to earn a living for many years to come, so take the long view toward the horizon where opportunity awaits. Then put pencil to paper.

These days few people can get by without a budget. If you're going into business for yourself, that's doubly true. Whether you use a software program or work out your budget categories on a yellow legal pad, be thorough.

- Go over your checkbook and through your recollections to determine your expenses for rent or mortgage payments, renters' or home insurance, auto payments and insurance, groceries, entertainment, health care, magazine subscriptions, morning coffee at Starbucks—whatever you spend money on.
- Figure what your first-year income should be.
- Cut your budget if your expenses are greater than your projected income.
- Bite the bullet, live within your budget, and monitor your success doing that each month.
- Put into savings at least 75 percent—preferably 100 percent—of any income you earn above your monthly projection. Good months and bad months will run together when you start out (see Tips 40 and 41) and often throughout the years that follow.

Do you need help planning a budget you can live with? Speak with your accountant or a financial planner. Or, for cheaper assistance, head for any library or bookstore. You'll find lots of money-savvy titles based on common sense. By all means anticipate that your income will be *lower* than you'd like and budget accordingly. Tighten your belt when you begin, and you can buy yourself time to fatten your business.

TIP 22

Feel right at home.

Find a dedicated private space for your home office, and furnish it with the right equipment.

There are excellent reasons to work at home, and not having to pay rent is only one of them. You will:

- Save time by not having to commute—and often sleep a little later in the bargain.
- Save the cost of commuting. You might even be able to jettison the second car and those insurance payments.
- Save the cost of more fashionable clothes and dry cleaning, since you can wear anything you wish while you work.
- Save lunch expenses by eating out of your refrigerator.
- Save additional money by possibly getting a tax break on the space you devote to your home office. Your accountant can fill you in on the ever-changing IRS regulations.

Be aware, however, that your home office can *cost* you money unless you arrange a space that's functional and private. You should also pay particular attention to Tip 23.

If you live alone, you'll have all the privacy you need. But be sure your work space is large enough to keep you from feeling physically and mentally cramped. It's one challenge to stay in your house all day and an even more serious one to stay in your bedroom, if that's where you place your desk. If you can turn the dining space in your kitchen or dining room into an office, do that and eat in the living room. Or turn your living room into an office and use it only secondarily for reading, listening to music, and watching TV.

Living with others will pose a whole new set of challenges and make designating a private work space a must. If you're using an extra room as a TV or guest room, make the sacrifice and turn it into your office. If not, search for space in your dining room, living room, family room, or garage.

If you can occupy only part of a room, consider using a screen or some other barrier to create a sense of separation. "White noise" from a sound machine or appropriate music can help filter out distractions.

What equipment and furniture will you need in your office? In 1979 my primitive desk, cardboard file cabinets, and manual typewriter hardly qualified me for a layout in *Architectural Digest.* But they proved functional, and they followed me into the home we bought in 1983 where I turned a breakfast room into my office.

(We had previously bid unsuccessfully on a home with a detached garage that would have made a dream office I might never have left.) In the few short years since then, office technology has been launched into another era. Today you'll probably need all or most of the following items:

- A desk or work surface large enough for a computer, modem, printer, and other peripherals like a scanner as well as space for writing, drawing, and doodling.
- An old typewriter if you find, as I do, that it's faster than your printer for addressing envelopes or if your handwriting has become indecipherable.
- A comfortable office chair. A spare kitchen or dining room chair may be cheap but self-defeating. The human back does not take well to prolonged sitting.
- A telephone, answering machine, and fax machine or some combination of those. Your fax should also make copies.
- A small copying machine.
- At least one two-drawer file cabinet. Computers have not eliminated paper; they've increased the uses for it.
- Shelves for reference books and office supplies.

Go with the 1970s philosophy that "I need my space," and in time you may be able to afford the space for a dedicated home office that your family, friends, and colleagues will envy.

TIP 23

Shape up or ship out.

Discipline yourself to work effectively by scheduling each day's activities and rationing life's little pleasures as rewards for tasks completed.

Now that I have a downtown office, I frequently take a long walk at lunchtime to break the routine. San Francisco is a great city to wander in, thanks to fabulous weather year-round (rainy days excepted) and so much to see. When I walk along the Embarcadero—a boulevard that runs along the Bay and offers great views of ferries and tankers, Treasure Island, the Bay Bridge, Oakland, and the East Bay Hills—I become envious. Runners abound, getting in terrific workouts in the middle of the day while I have to wait until I go home because there's no shower in my office. When I worked at home, on the other hand, I could run before lunch virtually whenever I wished.

There is, however, a flip side to the benefits of a home office, because it's possible to do anything you wish whenever you wish. No boss calls you when you don't show up at the office on time, so you can sleep late when you should be working. The refrigerator *does* call—usually throughout the day. Colleagues don't drop by to interrupt with "You've got to see this," but the VCR beckons you to drop out and watch the video you've waited months to get your hands on.

With distractions abounding and no supervisor to make demands on you, it's vital that you schedule your time and activity every day. Know what tasks and deadlines you're confronting (see Tip 18); then rough in how much time you'll devote to each and which time periods you'll spend doing them. If you've got several jobs going at once, the pressure may keep you going. But that same pressure can be fatiguing and provide an excuse to take one break after another until the pressure increases to the critical stage because you've fallen behind.

Rather than ignore distractions, incorporate them into your schedule! Want to take a break and enjoy that last piece of coffee cake? Make that your reward for completing and faxing the detailed estimate that's due by the end of the day. Want to relax with your favorite magazine, which just arrived in the mail? Preview it *after* you've updated your files or made all your client calls for the day. Want to head to the gym for a workout? Take on those Nautilus machines *after* you finish your bookkeeping and update your prospect list with ten new names.

You must also deal with the ultimate distraction—people. If someone else stays at home during the day, set clear ground rules from the start about when you're available and when you're not to be disturbed. Sure, you'll be delighted to talk about that new movie—but not until you've come up with at least five workable concepts for your new project. Want to go to a matinee? You can—but make sure you'll be allowed to work undisturbed in the evening.

Do you have children? I worked at home until our youngest child was ready for kindergarten. When all three kids were at school, my schedule went smoothly. When they got home, they wanted Dad's attention—and they got it. Usually. If I could, I set aside an hour or two of work time in the evening to make up for the time I spent with the kids. If that wasn't feasible, I explained that I could only say hello and admire a treasured drawing before going back to the task at hand. I spent a lot of valuable time with the kids that way, and I got my work done too.

Earn your breaks and you'll stay fresher and more relaxed even as you work harder.

TIP 24

Flee home when distractions become too great.

Not everyone finds home the best place to work. If you move to an outside office, you may easily offset its cost with enhanced productivity.

In 1988 a client of mine who had become a close business associate was faced with eviction. The small downtown building that housed his office and that of another small business had been rezoned for residential use. He asked me if I wanted to sublet space from him in another building since we worked on so many projects together. I said yes.

If working at home was so great, why did I agree to move my office out? There are several good reasons for working outside your home:

Distractions will always occur at home, no matter how disciplined you are. In your early years as a freelancer, you may have few jobs and plenty of time to enjoy being at home. But as your business grows, your need to maximize productivity will become a dollars-and-cents issue. You may find yourself working most nights, as I did, to make up for time spent with family during the day. At my new office there were no personal phone calls, no household chores beckoning, and no kids wanting to go to the park for batting practice.

Meetings can become doubly time-consuming. Phones, faxes, E-mail, and messengers have eliminated a lot of face-to-face client contact for freelancers. But you can't effectively seek new business or service the business you have without seeing people. If you live at any distance from your clients, a meeting can cost you an hour or two of travel time. Being at the edge of San Francisco's Financial District, only two blocks from the Transamerica Pyramid, I'm within a ten-minute walk of many of my clients. By staying close to your clients, you will save time when you have to get together, and you'll have a real competitive advantage. Clients do value your instant availability when only a face-to-face meeting will do. If you wish, of course, you can rent an office close to your home, minimize your daily commute, and simply take the extra time to get to clients' offices. This works best if meetings are generally few and far between.

Social isolation can become serious. When you work at home, you risk developing cabin fever by staying inside all the time. Furthermore you have no colleagues with whom to bounce ideas around or just share the day's news. You'll know you're too confined when a meeting becomes a treasured social occasion.

Working away from home can help you feel more professional. Believe me, there's nothing wrong with working out of your home. But considering the doubts some people express about freelancers, you may feel better about yourself if you have an office to go to. Also, your clients may be more impressed if you have an office, which represents permanence and commitment to your business—and theirs.

Renting an office costs money, but I never could have reached and surpassed the $100,000 income level at home. Raise your daily productivity, and you can raise your annual income.

TIP 25

Get the inside story on an outside office.

There's more than one way to find the right office in the right location. Whichever route you take, make information your first priority.

Subletting an office from an associate (see Tip 24) made a great deal of difference to my business, and it cost me very little. I gave my landlord a rent check on the first of each month. In return I received not only office space but also the services of a receptionist (we later switched to voice mail) as well as a printer, photocopy machine, and fax. I didn't even have to pay for paper. It was a wonderful deal but not necessarily an exceptional one.

You can, of course, lease an office long-term or rent one on a month-by-month basis. You can also lease or purchase all the equipment you'll need. In most cities and towns, there's enough office space from which to choose so that you can balance how far from home you'll have to go with how far from your clients you'll be.

If signing a lease makes you nervous, consider the alternatives:

Sublet from a client or other company with excess office space. It's amazing how many companies, large and small, have extra offices and would love to receive a modest monthly rental income to cover all or part of their expenses. Added advantages for you might include the use of office equipment, a conference room, and perhaps a prestigious address. Just as important, you may be able to strengthen an existing business relationship or establish a new one. Warning: sudden growth of your business or a strained relationship with your landlord could squeeze you out.

Rent or lease an office with one or more associates. Single offices are usually scarce or overly expensive. Two, three, or four people, however, can find and afford adequate space, often in a smaller building. Be aware, though, that the people with whom you share office space may not share your commitment to staying in business. Even one person bailing out could imperil your financial situation, and legal action can get very messy, not to mention expensive.

Check out offices in executive buildings that rent by the month or even by the day. Many businesspeople need an impressive address and someone to answer the phone but spend most of their time on the road. The rent in a building like this may be surprisingly reasonable, and you can generally walk away whenever you wish. Your rent may include the services of a receptionist. And virtually any type of equipment you'll need will be on the premises. Be aware that executive facilities do charge for most services—from use of a copy machine and voice mail to conference room and secretarial assistance. Review a detailed list of charges in advance, and then calculate the real bottom-line rent you'll be paying.

Wherever you locate your outside office, you'll need to add up some additional costs:

- A security system
- Insurance
- Painting or redecorating (you may be allowed to do it yourself)
- Installation of additional telephone lines for a dedicated modem or fax machine
- Installation of a voice-mail system.

Look around and examine all of the possibilities before you make a decision to rent an office. You'll be taking a small leap to another level, but you could also make giant strides toward building your business and your income.

Chapter 4

OPERATING EFFICIENTLY

Back in the sixties I read a magazine article that has continued to inspire me. A hod carrier in England became discouraged by the commonly accepted practice that had everyone work by himself and at the same slow pace, in spite of the fact that each worker got paid by the load rather than by the hour or the day. Seeing an opportunity, he approached a second hod carrier about teaming up and working as hard as they could. Hauling bricks at a construction site is no easy way to make a living, but this ambitious hod carrier, lacking education but not spirit, believed that by pushing harder and working smarter, he could increase his earnings significantly, improve his living standard, and eventually leave hod carrying altogether.

While others worked at a snail's pace and took ample time for smokes and tea, he and his partner found ways to get more done in tandem, then pushed, pushed, and pushed. After a few years the hod carrier purchased a $100,000 home in the country complete with horses and was planning to purchase a tea shop in town to which he could devote the rest of his income-earning years.

Looking back, it seems quite clear that this unskilled laborer was very skilled indeed. He understood the value of his time and found ways to make it as efficient and productive as possible. You can do the same—and do it a lot more comfortably, too.

TIP 26

Save mañana for vacations.

Organize your day around your work, and set goals you can reasonably achieve.

Having three children, I generally hear two familiar refrains at least once a day: "I'll do it later" and "I'll do it tomorrow." More often than not, later becomes tomorrow and tomorrow never comes. In the serious adult world of freelancing, however, a mañana philosophy can lead to grave problems. The services or skills you're selling are measured by the time you have to make them available. (For a different approach to time as it relates to charging fees, see Tip 43.)

Many employees buy into the myth of freelancing as a permanent vacation. What could be better than sleeping late, working on your screenplay, working out at the club, sipping caffè mocha while reading the newspaper, and occasionally doing some work? I'll tell you what succinctly: prospering!

Forget about having the freedom to stay in bed while your former coworkers are starting their commutes. Quality work takes time. So does finding that work. And so does maintaining relationships with the clients who provide that work. As an advertising agency employee, I arrived at the office by nine most mornings. Sometimes, of course, I went in later. I could get away with it. Wasn't I, as a "creative," someone special? Now, after nearly two decades as a successful freelancer, I'm usually at my desk by eight—and often by seven-thirty.

There are days when you may have little to do. Don't they offer the perfect opportunity to sleep in? The answer is no. You may be tempted to go into mañana mode when work is scarce, but that is precisely when you need to complete any tasks you have in case a client should call with a rush job; turn your attention to the reasons why you have so little work; and find more ways to market yourself effectively.

Yes, there are times when you can treat yourself to a few hours off. Going to a midday movie or stopping in at a museum is not a sin. But you'll do far better to view these diversions as occasional rewards rather than weekly routines.

Carve out a full workday, set consistent hours, and establish the habit of sticking to your schedule. With this mind-set, you'll be amazed at how much you really have to do—and how much time you have available in which to do it.

TIP 27

Back up to advance.

Save your computerized documents often, duplicate files as you quit them, and keep backups in your computer and in your office space as well.

When you're a teenager, danger doesn't exist. Once you get entrenched in adulthood, however, you begin to realize that your parents were right when they advised you to expect the unexpected and prepare for the worst.

On October 17, 1989, my son Seth and I sat in the upper deck at Candlestick Park enjoying the twilight sunshine. We eagerly awaited the start of the third game of the World Series between the Oakland A's and our San Francisco Giants. Shortly after five o'clock, I began to hear what I thought was the pounding of thousands of feet on the concrete deck—a not unusual overflow of fan energy seeking an outlet in anticipation of the game. The sound grew louder, but not until we started swaying did I realize that the vibrations I was hearing were caused by a major earthquake. The movement of the upper deck increased until we were rocking forward and backward on an amusement park ride minus the amusement. I silently prayed that the deck wouldn't go down, a catastrophe that could have easily caused thousands of deaths. Fortunately, the 'Stick's expansion joints absorbed the quake's energy and the stadium held, suffering no damage except the falling of one relatively small chunk of concrete—even though the Loma Prieta earthquake measured 7.1 on the Richter scale. More than sixty people were killed in the Bay Area, however. And while property damage was lighter than the national media reported, it was considerable nonetheless. Everyday life came to a halt. Fortunately, my business continued unaffected as the Bay Area picked up the pieces.

For a freelancer, a disaster of any size—from Mother Nature flexing her muscles to a short in your coffeemaker that causes a small fire in your home or office—can threaten the very survival of your business unless you prepare beforehand. And because your business is so dependent on technology, you must make safeguarding your software, hardware, and even the space you occupy, a priority.

Interestingly, the whims of technology often mirror nature's sometimes irascible side. Computers crash. Bugs emerge in software. E-mail servers get clogged. So begin your preparations with an awareness of the little things that can and do go wrong with some frequency.

Save your work continually as you use your computer. No matter how state-of-the-art, computers crash. The culprit could be anything from a bug in your system to a power outage caused by an overeager utility company worker digging into an underground power line—something that occurs with great regularity outside my office. A power surge can even occur when everything's supposed to be okay. Failure to save your files could cost you hours of hard work. Worse, you could miss a tight deadline. And no client, no matter how sympathetic, wants to suffer the embarrassment of missing a deadline of his or her own because *you* couldn't get back up to speed quickly. You may be innocent, but believe me, you will pay.

If you get too wrapped up in your work to save manually, see if your operating system or applications feature automatic saving. An associate of mine uses QuarkXPress for her design work and has her automatic save set to fifteen minutes. It really helps. I don't have that feature and don't need it since I've developed the habit of saving at intervals of no more than two or three minutes—whenever I pause to think or to review something I've written.

Back up your files. Imagine that you've just saved and quit your last file. Then your computer crashes, and it's going to be at least a day before your hard drive can be restored. You can rent another computer, of course. But how do you access the files you're working on? You'll want to back up every file on a disk—anything from a floppy to a Zip drive to a XyQuest. If you can put an automatic backup system to work, do it. I don't have one, so I back up each file right after I quit it and go to my desktop. Wait until five o'clock, and a crash at four could rob you of a day's work.

Secure access to a second computer. If your computer crashes, you'll still need to keep on working. For convenience (since I don't like to miss dinner with my family, I take extra work home) and for safety, I have two Macintosh computers—one in my office and another at home. Too expensive? Consider using a less expensive model as your hardware backup. As an alternative, make arrangements with someone you know who can make a computer available to you. Or contact a rental company *in advance* to see how quickly you can have the model you need. Depending on your workload, you can even rent by the hour at Kinko's or a similar service outlet.

Arrange for backup office space. A lot can happen outside your computer, too. Following the 1989 earthquake, my office building, which suffered no damage, was closed for several days until city inspectors could confirm its safety. No problem for me—I worked in my home office.

Does that mean you're always safe at home? Hardly. Only one year after the quake, a massive fire in the Oakland hills destroyed three thousand homes! If yours is a home office, find a place at least a mile away—the home of a friend or a relative, or the office of an associate—where you can store backup disks containing your complete files, including all your financial records. Store updated disks at least weekly (daily would be best), because a fire could virtually put you out of business. And household fires are common indeed! I take a diskette with me each evening and transfer its files into my home computer.

You may be able to set up shop at a friend's home, associate's office, client's office, or executive center. Develop a plan that will provide you with a computer and office furniture and equipment as well as telephone and fax lines, all at virtually a moment's notice.

No matter what kind of insurance you carry—life, health, disability, liability—make "operating" insurance a staple you can rely on. Anticipate the unexpected, and you can save a lot of grief while some of your competitors end up falling by the wayside.

TIP 28

Forget the Houdinis.

Don't pull a disappearing act. Make sure that your clients can always reach you. Then respond to their calls as quickly as possible.

At the beginning of the twentieth century, Harry Houdini became an American legend. Defying death, Houdini would often be bound in chains with multiple locks and then shut into a box or cabinet and suspended in water. Of course, when the box was pulled up, it would be empty. Houdini's disappearance would be one more great escape. Houdini's accomplishments were impressive, but they weren't magic. His was a dangerous act, but much of the danger was an illusion, since Houdini knew exactly what he was doing—tricks he artfully concealed.

I had the chance to find out how a famous illusionist amazes a crowd when my wife and I went to see Blackstone perform in New York. During the second act, I volunteered to go up on stage and participate in one of Blackstone's illusions. It involved several other volunteers binding his wrists with rope. Blackstone, in the tradition of Houdini, freed himself. Then, before we returned to our seats, he pulled my knotted tie right off my neck—while leaving my neck healthily intact.

I can't tell you how he did the tie trick (I promised not to), but I can say I enjoyed appearing on Broadway and learning how Blackstone unfettered himself from the rope around his wrists. Illusion and reality are not the same.

All this brings me to a simple point. Disappearing is easy. As a freelancer, you control your work schedule as few employees ever can. Unlike traveling salespeople, for example, you have no boss setting your itinerary and demanding a strict accounting of your time. On the other hand, you do have clients and prospects. If you disappear, so will they. The real trick is to seem to be available even when you're not.

I'll give away a few of my own not-so-secret secrets:

Answer your phone immediately. Voice mail and answering machines make it very tempting to let the phone ring while you're working. And without question there are times when you just can't stop what you're doing to respond to a call. But I've made it a rule to pick up the phone whenever possible, even when I'm writing. As far as my clients are concerned, I'm there when they need me. Instant communication makes clients feel more comfortable, and client comfort builds good relationships.

Answer your messages promptly. You can't always pick up the phone. And you're not always at your desk. But you can return calls as soon as possible to cut down on the time your clients spend waiting. If you hear a call go through to your voice mail or answering machine, stop as soon as possible and return it. When you return to your office and see that your message light is on, listen to your messages immediately, then return your calls before doing anything else. Freelancers can't afford to treat clients casually.

Check your messages when you're away from your office. At a client meeting? Check your messages. Crosstown for lunch? Check your messages. Home early? Check your messages as soon as you arrive. It's amazing how often you'll end up with jobs you might have lost if you'd delayed checking your messages by as little as an hour. Those "I know it's short notice but something just came up and you've got to help me out" fees abound, and they can be worth thousands of extra dollars to you each year.

Inform your clients when you'll be gone. You've planned a long weekend that includes spending Friday hitting the slopes or cruising the lake. Great. You've been working hard, and you've earned your playtime. Just make sure your clients know *in advance* when you'll be gone. (*Where* you're going is *your* business.) Yes, when you were a teenager, your parents used to ask you how long you'd be gone and when you'd return, and you hated it. But even when you disappeared to a friend's house or to the movies, they still loved you. Clients are not always that forgiving. It's not enough to leave a voice mail or answering machine greeting saying you'll be out of the office today. A client who expects you to solve a problem can cause you a bigger problem if he's upset by the fact that you're not available as expected. As the Holiday Inns used to say in their ads, "The best surprise is no surprise."

Make responding to your clients a major priority, even when it's not convenient. You'll create the kind of illusion that becomes a welcome reality to your clients and wins you additional business year after year.

TIP 29

Write it in stone.

Keep every promise and meet every deadline—or the other ninety-nine tips in this book can't help you.

The day before writing this chapter, I called a new client—referred to me by someone I knew—about two small invoices that were well past due. I was not pleased (for details on handling similar situations, see Tips 54 to 58), since I had done the work correctly, delivered it on time, and earned the client's compliments. What's more, both projects were rush jobs that had required me to put aside (though not miss deadlines on) other tasks. In return, I very rightly expected to be paid on time.

Now, let's flip that situation around. A client awards you a job, agrees on your fee, and intends to process your check on schedule after receiving your invoice. As a result, your client expects your work to meet predetermined guidelines and fulfill the objectives that have been set. Most of all, that client expects to receive your work when promised. It's up to you to stay with your client's schedule. But other clients, other jobs, and even personal matters can interfere. Here's how you can live up to your end of the bargain:

Be sure you understand a project's objectives and deadlines before concluding a client meeting or phone conversation. Guesswork can delay you or throw you entirely off the mark. Questions demonstrate intelligence and diligence, not stupidity. Ask away. (For advice on communicating in the middle of a project, see Tip 33.)

Review your work schedule to avoid making false promises. You can't promise to meet any one deadline without being fully aware of all your other responsibilities. Stay on top of your workload. (See Tip 18.)

When a rush job comes up, check your daily schedule to see if you've given yourself false deadlines. I generally target delivery dates for my work prior to a client's expectations. Clients appreciate a fast response, but they don't expect to receive the work before the agreed-upon deadline. In a pinch you can buy extra time fairly easily by moving *your personal completion dates* back to the original dates given to you.

Call another client to see if a deadline can be moved. There are times when a client can be flexible. I'm not talking about months or even weeks but often days. If you're honest about your need to work on another job, most clients will be cooperative, if they're not under the gun. Two warnings. First, don't please one client at the risk of losing another. No freelancer can afford to develop a reputation for unreliability since word gets around fast in any business community—New York, Chicago, and Los Angeles included. Second, don't make a habit of asking for extensions. Given the pressures in today's corporate world, clients can get very nervous if they suspect that you don't appreciate the expectations they face from their supervisors or bosses.

Make a crunch calendar (see Tip 32). You can increase your productivity and punctuality by organizing each day hour by hour when you have to juggle several deadlines at once. It works.

Follow up to see that client materials and input arrive as promised. It's impossible to do a job when you haven't been given the information you need. But it really won't help you to inform a client a week after the information was due that the memo, report, or graphic materials you were supposed to receive never arrived. Make no assumptions. Keep your eye on your client's responsibilities as well as your own. As soon as you spot a problem, call!

Honor your fee agreements. Clients have told me more than once about other freelancers who sent invoices for larger fees than had been agreed upon. Your written or oral estimate represents your word. If, while you're working on a project, a problem arises that leads you to believe you should be paid more, discuss the matter with your client *before* you send your bill. If the client changed objectives or the nature of the job, you'll probably work something out. If you did a poor job of estimating, however, be prepared to eat your losses. It's *your* responsibility to arrive at the right fee for every job you do. (More about this in Chapter 6.)

Remember, talent and skill are the basis of your freelance business, but they will take you no further than your reputation for integrity. Do what you say you'll do.

TIP 30

Add "no" to your vocabulary.

Pass on a job when you can't provide what a client or prospect needs—or the client can't provide it for you.

After World War II my uncle Harry received a loan from my father with which to purchase a small office supply company in New Jersey. Uncle Harry thought he could do a good job with the business, and he was right. Not long afterward he became a millionaire. Many years later he brought his son and son-in-law into the business. My cousin told me once how, despite his wealth, Uncle Harry would agonize over losing the smallest customer, even though his customers included major corporations. We laughed. But I well understand how Uncle Harry felt.

When you build a business from the ground up, every client or customer is important. The early fears always remain in your memory, as does the thrill of winning new clients and growing your business. That's why it's so difficult to turn down any job. But there are times when you must:

Say no when you can't meet a deadline. It's better to turn down a job with an honest explanation that you haven't the time than it is to be late. No healthy client relationship will suffer from the truth and your expressed concern for your client's well-being.

Say no when you haven't the expertise to do the job. Of course you want to stretch your talent and meet new challenges, but you need to be realistic about what you can and cannot do. Poor performance can be far costlier—both in the short term (your payment goes into limbo) and in the long term (your reputation plummets)—than declining when you know a project is beyond you. Moreover, recommending someone who is competent to do the job can earn you gratitude that will repay your forthrightness in the future.

Say no when you don't feel you can trust a client. Without question, you're going to go into a meeting every now and then and immediately sense that the chemistry is wrong. Possibly you hear the client berating an employee or a supplier. Bad sign! Maybe you pick up hints that the client's business dealings are dishonest. Danger ahead! Perhaps you sense that the client is fishing for ideas and isn't serious about doing business with you. Rip-off artist at work! Or maybe everything is fine until the subject of your fee comes up; then the gap between the client's offer and your needs is wide enough to drive a Humvee through. (You can add your own warning here: ___!) Over time, you will develop a sixth sense that will warn you off. Listen to it. Keep your eyes and ears open and enter into any new situation with a small but healthy touch of skepticism. When in doubt, bow out.

Say no when you're offered a job that will create a costly conflict with another client. Unless you are on retainer (see Tip 48), you have the right to work for an existing client's competitors. But the first client has an equal right, no matter how unfair it may seem, to cast you adrift if this becomes a sensitive point. And your relationship may well be severed forever. You may not be totally without hope, however. Because a client's notion of who his competitors really are can be broader than reality would indicate, you may be able to demonstrate that a perceived conflict doesn't really exist. Nonetheless, if a new piece of business is likely to cost you a greater volume of business with an existing, and perhaps touchy, client, pass on it—or accept gracefully your diminished billings and income.

Abraham Lincoln said, "You can't fool all of the people all of the time." From his own experience, he could well have added, "You can't please them all, either." Be honest with yourself, and you'll build a far stronger foundation for success.

TIP 31

Follow through.

Dot all the i*'s and cross all the* t*'s. Your professionalism will separate you from your competition.*

In Tip 4, I told a story about a fellow freelance copywriter who came up with an interesting but incomplete concept for a pizza chain's television commercial. I had to actually write the script for him since he couldn't make the concept work while meeting the client's retail selling needs and coming up with a satisfactory ending, all within the commercial's time limit of thirty seconds. For all his creativity, the impression he left with the person who hired him was negative. (He soon went back to work with an advertising agency where team members could pick up his loose ends.)

As a freelancer, you are responsible for accomplishing everything your client requests from you. That means paying attention to detail and presenting your finished project on time.

You'll have done the job right when you have:

- Covered all of your client's objectives
- Done all of the required research and background reading
- Called your client with any questions that came up
- Proofread and spell-checked your documents
- Made sure every page of a printed document is clean and wrinkle-free
- Noted orally or in writing any potential problems or additional opportunities at the time you present your work, if not before
- Developed solutions or recommendations that will work within your client's budget or other parameters.

Think of every project as a marathon in which it's not a fast start that counts but running every step of the more than twenty-six-mile course. Take pains with your work, and your clients will feel very good about you.

TIP 32

Develop a crunch calendar.

When you're swamped with jobs, assign all or part of a task to every hour in every working day—and evening. Keep to your schedule to stay in control.

Shortly after I started my first job with an advertising agency, I decided to attend graduate school at night. I liked the idea of getting a master's degree, and I chose English because it had been my undergraduate major. I also liked the idea of having the G.I. Bill pay my way. I decided to take three courses—nine units—each semester. The workload was really too much, but I was fortunate to be able to spend long lunch hours studying in the conference room. Moreover, my check from Uncle Sam not only covered my tuition and books but left enough over to almost pay for the rent on our apartment during the school year.

When finals drew near, I paid the price. I had to study every night and on weekends. But *what* to study *when?* I developed my first crunch calendar. I don't claim this to be a singular work of genius. I assume that many people do this. If you don't, you should. In an ideal world, you would work on one high-paying project at a time. When you finished one, you'd have a few days off before starting another. And the money would flow! In the real world, however, several jobs often come due at or near the same time.

The crunch calendar is a simple device for keeping yourself on track by assigning tasks either to day parts (morning, afternoon, evening) or to specific hours (9:00–10:00 A.M., 3:00–4:00 P.M., 8:00–9:00 P.M.). You need to take the following steps:

- Estimate the number of hours you will need to complete a job.
- Check your job schedule for due dates.
- Fill in your crunch calendar so you'll know when to work on each job.
- Revise your crunch calendar when your time estimates are off (under as well as over), when deadlines change, and when projects are completed.

A typical crunch calendar might look like this (I don't work on Friday night or Saturday, so I leave them blank):

	Mon	*Tue*	*Wed*	*Thu*	*Fri*	*Sat*	*Sun*
8-9A	Gray brochure	Brown proposal	Greene ad copy				
9-10A	Gray brochure	Brown proposal	Greene ad copy	Gray brochure	Greene revisions		White brochure
10-11A	Gray brochure	Gray brochure	Greene ad copy	Gray brochure	Greene revisions		White brochure
11A-N	Gray brochure	Gray brochure	Greene ad copy	Gray brochure	Brown newsletter		White brochure
N-1P							
1-2P	Greene ad roughs	Gold sell sheet	Redd mail package	Gold sell sheet	Brown newsletter		Brown revisions
2-3P	Greene ad roughs	Gold sell sheet	Redd mail package	Gold sell sheet	Brown newsletter		Redd revisions
3-4P	Greene ad roughs	Gold sell sheet	Redd mail package	Gold sell sheet	Brown newsletter		Redd revisions
4-5P	Greene ad roughs	Gold sell sheet	Redd mail package	Gold sell sheet	Weekly billing		Gray revisions
5-7P							
7–8P	Redd mail package	Redd mail package	Redd mail package	Brown newsletter			
8–9P	Redd mail package	Redd mail package	Redd mail package	Brown newsletter			
9–10P	Redd mail package	Redd mail package	Redd mail package	Brown newsletter			

How jobs are scheduled on your crunch calendar will depend on whether you deliver jobs in stages. I generally send clients concepts or copywriter's rough layouts with headlines first, then send the copy later. And the revision process can go on through several drafts, as agreed upon. So it may be impossible to dedicate one unbroken block of time (one, two, or more days without interruption) to a single job.

Use your crunch calendar, stay flexible, and check your progress against your deadlines. You can make the impossible very possible—and very profitable.

TIP 33

Keep your mind—and all the lines—open.

Be ready to improvise on short notice, and commit yourself to communicating whenever you recommend or implement a change.

One day in Officer Candidate School at Fort Benning, my company faced the challenge of a unique, and unforgettable, obstacle course. Instead of testing our physical strength, this course—consisting of ten fiendish obstacles incorporating walls, towers, and bodies of water—had been designed to stimulate our mental agility. As we began each new challenge, our instructors gave our squad of ten men (each man taking a turn as squad leader) an assortment of planks and ropes along with a ten-minute deadline and the caveat that no one could get wet!

Twenty-four squads were given one attempt at each obstacle. All failed. And for good reason. We rushed into every challenge enthusiastically but continually trapped ourselves in impossible positions. We then rushed into a second attempt and even a third, always hoping to find our way across or over the obstacle and always coming up short. We concluded the day more than a little frustrated and embarrassed.

Our instructors, however, informed us that we hadn't been expected to succeed. Rather, the course pointed out to us a simple but very effective lesson: evaluate your situation first, get suggestions from everyone, devise a plan, and then act, leaving enough time to make adjustments if necessary.

Why leave time to try again if you've come up with a sound strategy in the first place? Because in the real world, few undertakings go as planned. That's especially true in war, which is why the army so highly values an officer's ability to improvise. But effective improvisation requires several key qualities: the ability to recognize a changing situation; the willingness to accept the change; the determination to think through alternatives, often very quickly, before acting; and the understanding that a new plan must be communicated before it can be put into effect.

An afternoon commute can provide a perfect example of a situation requiring improvisation. Traffic is stop-and-go, with more stop than go. You'll be late for dinner, and friends are coming over. You could curse, scream, and pound your horn, but that won't make traffic move any faster. So instead, you turn your radio to the traffic report and find out that the freeway is blocked by an accident several miles ahead. You start moving over to the right as you evaluate alternative routes, select one, and exit as soon as possible. Then, since you'll be late, you turn on your cell phone or pull over to a phone booth and call home.

In Tip 29, I advised you to ask questions and obtain resource materials before you begin a project. You want to create an efficient, productive plan before you begin. But often you may have to improvise after you've gotten started. Your client has a change of mind. A competitor upstages your client. Your budget changes. Expected resources dry up. New resources suddenly become available. A personal or family problem demands your attention and threatens a deadline.

Stay flexible. Clients truly appreciate your support when you rally behind their attempts to solve problems. Stay calm. Complaining wastes energy and precious time. Change requires your clearest thinking. Stay committed. When you have an idea you believe will improve a project after you've begun working on it, feel free to offer your suggestion with all the supporting facts. Give your client the option of accepting or rejecting your recommendation. And always *stay in touch.* Call, fax, or E-mail everyone involved in your project when any change must be made for any reason.

Improvisation and communication go hand in hand. Some of the most brilliant improvisers become loose cannons when they fail to get the word out. Just bear in mind the comment made by the vicious warden in regard to the suffering chain gang in the Paul Newman movie *Cool Hand Luke:* "What we've got here is a failure to communicate."

Chapter 5

MANAGING THE MONEY SIDE

Workday mornings I browse the newspaper as I eat breakfast, first checking the main news, then going to the sports and business sections before reading a comic strip or two. While sports and business are kept separate, sports fans know that they are very much linked. Athletes and dollars are bound together and not, in my opinion, very much for the good. But the situation provides two very good examples every freelancer should bear in mind.

I once read about two players with the New York Yankees—my favorite team as a kid—during the championship years of the fifties. Each was in the starting lineup, and each made a comparable contribution to the team's success. In those days, before free agency, teams basically dictated players' contracts. Every winter one of the two players routinely received his annual contract, signed it, and dropped it in the mail. The other held on to his contract, countered with a higher figure, and made enough of a fuss to get an increase of a few thousand dollars. The Yankees didn't mind, and the player came away with extra money. Those veterans' salaries were only a fraction of today's *minimum* salaries for rookies, and the few thousand dollars extra the second player was able to generate made a real difference to his family.

Fast-forward to professional basketball in the early nineties when the escalation of sports salaries had become bewildering. A high first-round draft choice of the Golden State Warriors, whom I began following when I moved to San Francisco, ended up broke only a few years after signing a multimillion-dollar contract. Stories of wealthy athletes losing their fortunes abound.

Taking responsibility for the financial side of your freelance business poses no different an obligation than keeping your personal finances in order. True, it can seem like an overwhelming task because it demands shedding many of the illusions that surround freelancing (see Tips 1–7). The fact is that freelancers, rather than shedding unwelcome tasks imposed by employers and supervisors, often have to accept additional roles. For many people, dealing with money is a challenge on which they'd rather pass. But to become a $100,000 freelancer, you have to wear the hat of chief financial officer along with all the others on your head.

While virtue as its own reward is an exemplary premise from a moral and ethical perspective, remuneration represents a key reward in business. Business is about profit—not profit at someone else's expense, mind you, but profit based on hard, honest work and a just return for your efforts. Only by profiting appropriately can you *stay* in business, maintain your independence, and provide for your family and your future.

A very talented illustrator I knew in San Antonio put it quite succinctly, and honestly, when he included on his business card the slogan "*Ars Gratia Pecuniae*"—art for money's sake.

TIP 34

Build it—and they will come.

Set ambitious but achievable goals for your monthly and annual billing.

In the movie *Field of Dreams,* Kevin Costner, a big fan of old-time Chicago White Sox baseball great Shoeless Joe Jackson, builds a lighted diamond in the middle of an Iowa cornfield. His project is a direct response to a voice that tells him, "If you build it, he will come." Indeed, the spirit of Shoeless Joe, who protests his innocence in the 1919 World Series gambling scandal, does appear, followed by his teammates. At the end of the movie, Costner's character meets his own father as a young catcher in the prime of life. The two play catch silently—a very American father-son bonding ritual. Costner is then rescued from bankruptcy (no corn grows on his superb—and expensive—ball field) when his young daughter informs him that people will come and buy tickets. The movie ends with a seemingly endless stream of vehicles approaching the farm at nightfall to visit this baseball wonder. (The field built for the movie has been a popular attraction ever since.)

Kitsch? Maybe. But the movie really does offer a powerful lesson: goals precede achievements. *Solo Success* suggests the possibility of earning $100,000 a year as a freelancer. But as a freelancer you will not reach that income level as a matter of course. You have to target that goal first and then put in the effort that will push you toward it.

When I started freelancing, I set an income goal of $20,000 for my first year. That was lower than the salary I would have made as an employee, but I was starting from scratch. It seemed achievable. At year's end, I had come close, making $18,000. Falling short of a goal is perfectly acceptable—as long as you've set the right goal.

During my second year, I broke my annual income goal into monthly *billing* goals. Having developed a sense of what work I could command, I decided that fees of $2,000 a month would grow my business modestly and provide sufficient income. That second year, I billed $28,000, which was $4,000 over my target. When I first billed $3,000 in a month, I thought I'd performed a small miracle. If I could reach that goal each month, I'd be doing really well. It took another two years of effort not only to reach but to exceed that figure. (Today I would view a $3,000 month as a disaster.)

Through the years, I not only increased my monthly goals but *forced* myself to meet them (see Tip 45 for more). You can do the same when you adhere to the following principles:

Challenge yourself. A passive approach to fees and income can doom you to remain on the same income level year after year. It can also erode your financial well-being as inflation, no matter how small, chips away at your purchasing power. Then there's the danger of a "take it as it comes" philosophy leading to a shrinking business. Clients come. And clients go. A freelance business that fails to grow larger will often become smaller if it does not aggressively build existing client relationships and replace lost clients. Tip 7 discusses developing carrots—small rewards—to enhance your skill performance. Billing goals create the carrots that impel you to raise your financial performance.

Set goals that are realistic. If you're billing $2,500 a month in fees now, targeting $10,000 a month for next year might be admirable but foolish. Failure to achieve your goals can be discouraging. A 10 or 20 percent annual increase can lift your income dramatically over only a few years. And that kind of goal (it's not a formula, mind you) is achievable. Set your goals three to five years in advance. Then move forward at a reasonable but progressive pace. If business expands faster than anticipated, reevaluate your goals—even if that means arriving at more modest increases or even *temporarily* maintaining your billing level to adjust for unexpected opportunities that may not be repeatable.

Stay committed if you fall short. My third-year billings remained flat at $28,000. I was stunned and disappointed. But then I realized that I was in a transition period, transferring my workload from the advertising agency I had left (almost all my billings in year one) to other clients. I stayed with it, and my fourth-year billings hit $48,000, a 70 percent increase. Further, my billings kept going up from there. What happens when you challenge yourself to raise your billings from $30,000 to $35,000 and you bill $33,500? You still enjoy an increase of over 10 percent and raise the bar for the next year. Without that goal, you might never have achieved that increase.

Take a proactive stance toward all of the components of your freelance business—your monthly and annual fees, your client base, the kinds of jobs you'll do, and even the lifestyle you'll lead—and you'll go more than halfway toward succeeding.

TIP 35

Invest in number one first.

Put enough money into your business to get it going and keep it going.

Good friends of mine came to the United States from the former Soviet Union in 1989. They knew no English and virtually nothing about the American way of life. Yet they've prospered. True, they brought intelligence and education with them. But they also possessed great determination and the willingness to forgo immediate pleasures for future success.

Both Yury and Svetlana spent their first year in San Francisco studying English virtually all day. (I was assigned to them one night a week through a volunteer tutoring program.) Svetlana, who had been a high school science teacher, became a pharmacy technician, as she had been many years before in Ukraine.

Yury, unable to find a suitable engineering job, embarked on a new career importing textiles from Eastern Europe—a freelance occupation conducted in association with people who knew the specialty linen market here. He put a small amount of money into his first deal, made a profit, then put that profit into the next deal. When problems arose at textile plants, he invested in trips to Russia, Ukraine, Belarus, and Lithuania. He still travels there, for a month at a time, several times a year. Yury has done well in a short time because he remains in his modest home and is careful about such expenditures as cars and vacations. He learned quickly that in our capitalist system it takes money to make money, and Yury puts most of his profits back into his business.

I opened my freelance business back in August 1979 on a shoestring (see Tip 14 about budgeting for your first office). Of course, I was selling a service, not tangibles, so my initial expenses were low. But I invested in what I needed to get started. As my business grew, I upgraded my equipment from a portable typewriter to an IBM Selectric. Today you can get a laptop computer for less. My first computer, a Macintosh connected to a daisy wheel printer, followed. Not long after, I purchased a laser printer—a used one. It cost more than my first car—a *new* one. But it dramatically improved the appearance—and quality—of my printed work and enabled me get more done in less time.

Over the years I've invested in furniture for my home office, upgraded my business cards and letterhead, and kept pace—albeit modestly and often as a late adapter—with new technology.

While it's always tempting to put money into a trip to Hawaii or an adventure in the stock market, you need to make your freelance business your first investment option. And do this not just when you begin but throughout your business lifetime. You'll have three goals:

Maintain your professional image. Everything from your business card, letterhead, and other printed and promotional materials to the clothes you wear will make a powerful first impression. If you're a marketing consultant, you need suits to match your ambitions. If you're a graphic designer, you need enough computer memory to run the latest software and a good color printer to save money and time sending work out to service bureaus.

Increase your productivity. There are always a few old pros around who lament the passing of the typewriter. If you're lucky, they'll even show you their favorite quill pen. As a freelance copywriter, I could never do the volume of work at the high level of quality both my clients and I demand without word-processing capabilities. If you're a space planner who spends a lot of time at clients' offices, you'll rely on a top-of-the-line answering machine or voice mail. If you develop video games, you can't work without the fastest Internet and E-mail access available.

Seek, win, and keep business. There are times when it takes more than a phone call to attract a prospect. In fact, it's often terribly difficult to get through on the phone at all—and make an impression when you do get through, if you're calling cold (see Chapter 9). Moreover, keeping a client can be just as difficult (see Chapter 10). After all, you're not the only one selling your service. Your investment in new business and client relations may range from a first-class postage stamp on an envelope bearing a personal note to lunch at a hot new restaurant to a flight across the country (don't count on discount fares at short notice) complete with presentation-equipment rental, car rental, and hotel room.

A balanced "it takes money to make money" philosophy reflects a suitably aggressive posture toward success. Put part of your profits aside monthly for future self-investment—and invest in your freelance business *first* when funds are limited. You'll give clients all the right reasons to invest in you as well.

TIP 36

Become a bean counter.

Examine your expenses with an eagle eye, and prepare for financial challenges by keeping your lifestyle modest.

Who says there's no such thing as a free lunch? In my agency days in San Francisco, I was given close to carte blanche to take out any client, employee, or vendor in order to keep relationships running smoothly. I enjoyed a lot of free lunches on my expense account with never a question. When I went to Las Vegas to shoot TV commercials for a client there, I always took my director and talent to dinner and a show. After all, I was spending someone else's money.

Those days ended when I started spending my *own* money.

Open your freelance business, and part of you becomes a member of that frequently derided group of people whose sole mission in life seems to be thwarting your every opportunity—bean counters. You know who these folks are. They're the ones who always ask, "Do you need this? Can you do without this? Is there an alternative? Can you get it for less? Why do these things always cost so much?"

Money well spent represents a sound investment indeed. But any way you look at it, money spent is also an expense. How do you strike the right balance?

Set a budget and reevaluate it periodically. There *is* a difference between investing and squandering. Determine your expense limits as monthly figures or as a percentage of monthly gross. Mine comes to under 8 percent and is often as low as 4 percent when revenue is up. At the outset, of course, your expenses may represent a higher percentage of your gross income than they will when your business is on a roll. And your budget needs may change. Play devil's advocate over every expenditure.

Track your expenses continually. Cutting spending on the last day of your fiscal year is like locking the barn door after your horse has escaped. Refer back to Tip 19 and set up a system that lets you see all your expenses to date at a glance so your spending can be stopped on a dime when you've hit your limit.

Avoid bells and whistles. Technology is one of the key factors in promoting freelance success. Computers, modems, E-mail, voice mail, and the Internet all contribute. But they all cost, too. Just as in buying a car, it's easy to overspend. Find the middle ground between getting just the technology you need now and preparing for new technology tomorrow.

Consider leasing instead of buying your next computer. Technology and obsolescence go hand in hand. Today you may have more memory than you need. Tomorrow you'll end up installing additional memory or shopping for a new computer. Since hardware loses value fast—and hardware prices keep coming down—you'll probably get only a small percentage of your purchase price when you sell. Look into leasing. You'll pay as you go and be able to upgrade when the lease term ends.

Rein in your lifestyle. I once attended a seminar at which someone asked about cutting expenses after the loss of a major client and a subsequent major decline in revenue. The speaker thought for a while and then mentioned such solutions as canceling magazine subscriptions. The questioner wasn't satisfied; neither was anyone else in the room. And the speaker admitted his own frustration. But the answer is obvious: the time to cut spending is *before* a downturn in business. Put money aside for operating expenses monthly. And put reserves aside each month for emergency living expenses as well. Most important, see that your lifestyle lags behind your income. That way you won't have to even think about canceling subscriptions.

Ask yourself the basic questions every time you consider any purchase. Do I need this? Can I do without this? Is there an alternative? Can I get it for less? Why do these things always cost so much?

Balance your need to invest by stimulating the bean counter portion of your personality, and you'll stimulate the welcome combination of sound business growth and peace of mind.

TIP 37

Put your perks together.

Set up your benefits program to provide for unexpected emergencies.

In the nineties, benefits, not salary, became the key lure for corporate employees. Given the high cost—and sometimes the lack of availability—of health insurance, medical plans (with dental and vision plans as major pluses) often supplant salaries and bonuses as inducements to choose or stay with an employer, although federal law will make health insurance portable for many workers. For freelancers, the issue of benefits remains challenging. No one will supply them except you.

I must say up front that the situation is not perfect. As a freelancer, you really do *pay* for your benefits. But that's fine considering that (a) freedom always involves trade-offs; (b) many employees now share the cost of their benefits, so benefits are free for only a very few; and (c) you can take advantage of tax breaks to lower your benefit costs.

Health insurance. A major accident or illness can wipe out your savings and even leave nasty debts in their place. Your options include standard fee-for-service plans like Blue Cross or any number of health maintenance organizations (HMOs). Suggesting the right health plan is beyond my expertise, but there's no question you should be covered. And you *can* be.

- Be aware that as a freelancer, you can write off a portion of your health coverage premiums—40 percent in 1997 rising to 80 percent by 2006.
- Consider a high deductible with a fee-for-service plan to lower your premiums. I view my health plan as disaster coverage for major hospital stays, and I pay for doctor visits and lab tests (Blue Cross reduces most of these fees) as I do other bills. My deductible has never kicked in, but I'm very satisfied, since I can live with my bimonthly premium.
- Look for group coverage rates through business, alumni, fraternal, and religious organizations. They may offer substantially lower premiums on quality coverage. But be sure to research such coverage thoroughly!
- Check out the tax-advantaged Medical Savings Account that Congress put into effect on January 1, 1997. An MSA allows you to make a tax-deductible contribution to a special account

used for paying out-of-pocket medical expenses. You need a high deductible to qualify, and there may be a limit on the number of people who enroll. But the advantages look appealing. Because MSA contributions are tax-deductible, you decrease your tax burden while paying out-of-pocket medical expenses at *less* than one hundred cents on the dollar. What's more, interest earned is tax-deferred, and you can withdraw whatever is left at age sixty-five without penalty, paying taxes then on only the amount you withdraw. Again, speak with your accountant.

Life insurance. If you're single, you can hold off on getting life insurance if no one depends on you for financial support. If you're married and your spouse works, perhaps he or she can live on his or her income alone. Or maybe you want a small policy to help ease the transition after your death. On the other hand, if one income won't be sufficient for your survivor, or if you have children, you'll want to protect your family. You'll have to decide whether you want lower-cost term insurance, which has no investment value, or some other insurance option such as universal life or whole life, which build cash value. And you'll have to face the fact that your premiums won't be deductible. But adequate employer-paid life insurance is hard to come by, too. Like any employer, you pay for this coverage. Unlike other employers, you have to pay for only *one* person's coverage. Make it part of your benefits package.

Disability insurance. This is a tough one. If you're young, you are more likely to be seriously injured or ill than you are to die. And some people do become disabled. The good news is that disability insurance covers you when you can't work. The bad news is that you often have to be out of work for three months or more before you receive payments—meaning you must have adequate savings on hand. Also, your policy may contain a number of clauses that further limit your ability to collect. And disability coverage isn't cheap. Talk to your accountant or some other trusted financial adviser.

Long-term care insurance. Here's another difficult decision, particularly since your premiums will not be tax-deductible. A significant percentage of people age sixty-five and up will need nursing home or in-home care at some time. If you're poor, you may be able to rely on government assistance. If you're well off, your estate can probably absorb the costs. If your retirement income and estate are modest, however, long-term-care insurance could be a good idea, and premiums are relatively low when you're young. Again, speak with your financial adviser.

Aggressively assemble a package of perks that meets your needs; then evaluate it yearly. You'll benefit throughout the years to come.

TIP 38

Get ready to stop working.

Establish a retirement plan that takes advantage of major tax breaks to let you build an impressive nest egg.

When I was ten years old I had a terrific illustrated book about manned space flight. I looked at it, of course, as pure fantasy. A man on the moon? That was way off in the unforeseeable future. Only fifteen years later I watched as Neil Armstrong took his televised first step down to the moon's surface. Similarly, when I graduated from college, my father suggested that I might want to work for Sears because it had a great retirement plan. No twenty-two-year-old is interested in retirement. But now my sister, Kay, is a grandmother. And I'll be eligible for Social Security retirement benefits in fewer years than the gap between my book on space flight and the Apollo 11 mission.

Face it. You're going to get older, and there's no way that Social Security—if it survives along with you—will cover your condo on Maui, your country club membership, and an occasional round-the-world jaunt when island fever sets in. That's why setting up a self-employed retirement plan makes so much sense.

It's a win-win situation, because the contributions you make to your self-employed retirement plan are tax-deductible, and the interest and dividends you earn are tax-deferred. Result? A sizable chunk of your plan contributions represents money that would otherwise have gone to the government. You pay *no* taxes until you actually start withdrawing money, from as early as age fifty-nine and a half. And you may be able to withdraw your funds without penalty for a variety of reasons, depending on congressional legislation. Here's what I suggest:

Check with your accountant. Find out about the right plan for you, and ask about the maximum amount you can contribute each year. Bear in mind that you can contribute less than the maximum—or even nothing—if you wish. See how much you'll save in taxes, too. That should spur you on in a hurry.

Develop reasonable investment guidelines. During your younger years you'll want to take a growth-oriented approach. The risks are greater, but you've got adequate time to turn your losses around. And most reasonable investments do quite well over the long haul. As you get older, you'll swing your approach to the conservative side, minimizing risk. Bear in mind that you don't have to put all of your money into a single account—or a single kind of account. You can select certificates of deposit for one portion, mutual funds for another, individual stocks for a third, and so on. Do be aware that you won't benefit from normal tax-deferred investments like municipal bonds or Treasury bills, since your retirement fund interest and dividends are already deferred.

Seek assistance in developing your strategy if financial thinking isn't your forte. Books abound. Newspapers and magazines are full of advice. You'll find plenty of software on the subject, too. And if you'd like to take a more personal approach, look for an investment counselor with experience helping other people manage their money. You'll want to choose a counselor who charges a fee for developing a plan, and perhaps for analyzing it periodically, but who *never* sells any type of investment. You want totally objective advice only.

Determine your annual contribution goal in advance. Then make part of that contribution *each month.* Wait until April 15, and you might find yourself short of funds and miss a great opportunity. If you have extra money available before the April 15 deadline, of course, you can make an additional contribution and transfer more of the money earmarked for taxes to your future.

Put money into your retirement fund today so that you can retire in comfort tomorrow—no matter how far off that tomorrow is.

TIP 39

Write your annual report.

Analyze your bottom line and the way you're doing business when you close your books each year.

My daughter, Rachel, and my younger son, Aaron, liked to play a special game when they were small. They would close their eyes, hold my hand, and ask me to lead them through our neighborhood or the park. That game reflected a great deal of trust since they often went a long way with their eyes shut. As a freelancer, however, you have to find your way through each year with your eyes open.

Since *writing* provides the best tool for disciplined thinking, I strongly suggest that you create quarterly profit-and-loss statements and a year-end annual report that evaluates where you are as a company and where you're headed.

In your ledger (see Tip 19) keep monthly and year-to-date figures on revenues, expenses, net profits, and fees. You can see at a glance how you're doing against your goals and how the current year compares to the past one. This way you'll be prepared should your income go up faster than you anticipated, and you can call your accountant for advice regarding taking deductions sooner and revising your quarterly tax payments.

At year's end, check all the numbers, and ask yourself these questions:

- Is my income up or down?
- Were my fees larger or smaller?
- Did I have unexpectedly large expenses, and might they be repeated?
- Which clients contributed how much to my billings?
- Did I do as much business with each client as I expected?
- What are reasonable goals to set for the following year?

Then start writing. Of course, your annual report will probably have an audience of only one—you. But invest sufficient time to analyze your freelance business not only from the standpoint of quantity—fees, income, and expenses—but from that of quality as well. In simple, declarative sentences, describe:

- How your fees and income stack up with those of years past
- New clients you've attracted—and why
- Existing clients you've maintained—and why
- Clients you've lost—and why
- The strengths and weaknesses of the services you provide
- Ways in which you can improve the quality of your work
- New opportunities for expanding your range of services
- New possibilities for marketing yourself
- Your level of satisfaction—or dissatisfaction—with your performance
- The outlook for the future.

Be objective, concise—and ruthless. Then use your annual report to write your business plan for the coming year (see Tip 12).

And *act* on it. Get a firm grip on your progress, and you'll get a firmer grip on success.

TIP 40

Keep your head up in the valleys.

When business is slow, attend to unfinished chores, make new contacts, and above all, keep the faith.

If you're familiar with Adam and Eve, you know that this early tale in the Book of Genesis involves more than a man and a woman, a serpent, and a command not to eat a piece of fruit. The story is an important response to an eternal question: Why is life so hard?

I enjoy the deeper theological and philosophical discussions that surround this story, but the only response that fits within the range of this book is "Because that's the way it is." Recognize that hardship exists, anticipate it, and deal with it.

Freelancers face the same challenges that confront all businesses. At times things just don't go well. Clients stop calling or don't respond to your calls. Work flow is reduced to a trickle. Bills come in. Cash goes out. Funds seem to make a beeline toward depletion. You chart your billings and income, and the good months seem less like peaks than insurmountable obstacles that you can never climb again. You wonder why you ever gave up being an employee.

Cheer up! You're not alone. We all go through these periods. The billing-and-income charts of my early freelance years, when a few big jobs could skew the whole picture, look like the famed dragon's teeth mountains of southern China. In relationship to each other, the good months look very good. The bad months decline precipitously. But as the years passed, those charts began to take on a new shape. First, the peaks and valleys began flattening out as my business became more consistent. Second, the plane on which these peaks and valleys show themselves rose steadily as my income increased. The slopes grew gentler and the altitude higher. When compared, the bad months in the later years tower over the good months in the early years.

Even today I have an occasional month that leaves me wondering. But that month is still better than any I'd dreamed of when I started freelancing. More important, experience has taught me that business is cyclical in spite of my best efforts. Some bad months are virtually unavoidable. But good months will follow—as long as you maintain your commitment and effort.

How can you get through the valleys relatively unscathed?

Budget modestly. You'll handle rough times much more easily without the terrible pressure of worrying about paying your bills (see Tip 36).

Do all those little jobs you've been putting off. Clean up your desk and office. Weed out and reorganize your files. Bring your books up to date. Refresh your marketing materials and develop new ones. Reevaluate your business processes and write a plan for the next month, quarter, and year.

Look for new business. Yes, the phone has a way of ringing after a dry period. But you, as a freelancer, have to make your own breaks. Luck is simply readiness to seize an opportunity. Moping around with time on your hands is self-defeating. Contact existing clients. Sending a newspaper clipping relative to a client's work responsibilities or personal interests is a great way to keep your name out front. Develop your prospect list and start making calls. Then follow up those calls with letters or mailers. Let associates and friends know you're looking for more business—doing fine, mind you, but always seeking to grow (see Chapter 9 for details).

Cut yourself some slack. There are times when nothing seems to work. Keep your cool—and your confidence. When you really need a lift, treat yourself: spend the morning reading the entire newspaper in your favorite coffeehouse, enjoy a long walk in the park at midday, or take in an afternoon movie. Remember, none of us have complete control over the cycles we go through.

What do I do when I descend into a valley? All of the above. (I actually have gone to one afternoon movie.) And a bit more. I carried the idea for this book around with me for several years until I hit a valley, found myself with unexpected time, saw an opportunity, and began writing. As I was really getting into it, business suddenly got hot. When I found myself in another small valley, I wrote a proposal and worked up the courage to send it to a number of publishers. And yes, business started flooding in right afterward.

When you feel you're down as far as you can go, pick yourself up and pick up chores you've dropped by the wayside. You'll be ready to pick your business up when the ground begins to rise.

TIP 41

Stay grounded on the peaks.

Hold a modest celebration to mark each success, put extra money away, then roll up your sleeves to stay on top.

I well remember how startled—and delighted—I was the first time I billed $10,000 in fees in a single month. I honestly would not have believed it possible when I left my advertising agency job to freelance. Hitting $20,000 in a month was equally amazing to me. The few times I've hit the $30,000 level still leave me shaking my head in wonderment. The experience is dizzying. But this experience has also taught me that this kind of success doesn't last forever.

Win a major job, hit an "impossible" milestone, or receive an unbelievably large check, and you've really accomplished something. By all means, celebrate. It's important to reward yourself for your hard work. But just as road builders often "cut and fill" to level hills and smooth the ride, savvy freelancers no more go overboard after good months than they become despondent after bad ones. Aristotle's golden mean applies to business as well as anything else.

How do you make a great month work *for* you instead of against you?

Stash a larger amount in your tax fund. Based on your previous year's income, a couple of great months could kick you into a higher tax bracket (see Tip 20). You'll be paying a higher percentage of your income, so your existing tax formula could leave you short. Give your accountant a call if need be. And remember that any surplus in your tax fund is yours to keep. You can roll those extra dollars over to cover your next tax year or transfer some of that money to your retirement or savings accounts.

Add to your savings. It's tempting to spend extra cash right away. But it's also dangerous. You need a cushion for the bad months, and you can build it during the good ones. Save first. Spend later.

Invest in your business. Extra income offers the perfect opportunity to build your freelance infrastructure (see Tip 35). Whether you need a new or upgraded computer, an expensive software program, more letterhead, or a better capabilities brochure, use your windfall to maintain your momentum.

Add more to your savings.

Take a reality check. You *should* feel proud of a good month. You should also avoid unrealistic expectations. Yes, your business will grow if you're good at what you do and if you pay attention to these tips. But let your expectations be grounded in confidence, not cockiness. The clients who adore you today can easily go out of business tomorrow—or transfer their affections to someone else. And chances are that sooner or later, they will.

Roll up your sleeves and work harder. You know how much effort it took to have that great month? It will take even more effort to duplicate it. Climbing the mountain is hard. Creating a plateau in that relatively thin, yet rich, air is even harder. Rededicate yourself.

Stay objective when you achieve a fabulous success so that you can continue to meet your objectives for future success.

TIP 42

Follow the money.

Keep pace with business trends and information that can drive your profits up.

Some years ago I attended a seminar presented by two former advertising agency executives on the business of running a small agency. As a contented freelance copywriter, I had no desire to form my own agency or enter into an agency partnership. But I believed that parts of the seminar would be appropriate for me. I also believed that if I walked away with one valuable tip, I could be repaid many times over for the cost of the fee and my time.

One piece of advice from that seminar has stuck with me over the years: "Bill on estimate." The object of this strategy is to enhance cash flow by getting paid as soon as possible. I'll cover my own approach to this practice in Tip 50. But I'll say here that the general principle involved has paid for itself many times over—and that simple tip cost me many times more than this book cost you.

To stay on top of your business, you must continually absorb new information apart from that relating to the skills that apply to your specific freelance service. Several sources are readily available:

Look for seminars relating to running freelance, micro (up to five employees), or home businesses. Professional and university groups frequently offer these workshops. But do check the credibility of the presenters. You want to learn from people who have practical experience, not theorizers. And do think of these seminars as *investments,* not expenses. Pick up that one valuable tip, and you *will* make money—possibly lots of it.

Take a basic bookkeeping or accounting course. Even if you plan to use a bookkeeper, you need to know what he or she will be doing. Furthermore, you need to be able to discuss your bookkeeping and tax records intelligently with your accountant. As an undergraduate I took two semesters of accounting to meet my general requirements. I'm no expert, but I do understand the basic principles and I used them to set up my own inelegant but highly functional books. As chief financial officer, you must know how to track and evaluate money coming in and money going out.

Read the business section of your newspaper. From time to time you'll find information on businesses and industries similar to yours and the way they market themselves and solve problems. You'll also find tips on taxes, bookkeeping requirements, helpful software, and business banking.

Browse continually for helpful books and magazines. No, you don't have the time to read everything. But yes, good information is constantly being published. As long as you remain aware and receptive, you'll find other money-saving and money-making tips throughout your freelance life.

It definitely bears repeating that one piece of sound information could prevent you from losing thousands of dollars or enable you to add thousands to your bottom line—year after year.

Accept your financial role and seek out new knowledge. Before you know it, you'll be enjoying greater rewards.

Chapter 6

DETERMINING FEES AND RATES

A professional basketball player can score $10 million a season—over $120,000 a game, not including playoff money. A movie star can command $20 million for a single film. (The movie may be a dog, but the financial coup seems worth applauding.) And a heavyweight fighter can sock away $30 million for a bout that might last less time than it takes most of us to draw water from the cooler. So how much are *you* worth?

In a free market, not two but three entities determine the value of your work. Obviously you and your client will negotiate your fee. Sometimes your client has the upper hand: you have lots of competitors; she's been given a budget chiseled in granite. Sometimes you prevail: a tight deadline looms; there's a lack of talent available. But an additional player enters the game. Your industry usually dictates the basic financial parameters within which anyone can expect to work.

Sports, entertainment, and literature, for example, offer athletes, performers, and writers the opportunity to make huge amounts of money—sums that keep growing seemingly beyond the imagination—if they possess either the talent, or fame, or notoriety necessary to excite paying customers. Teachers, nurses, and carpenters work in fields whose pay scales are dramatically lower and rise only slowly. Like it or not, free market forces dismiss individual and social worth. It's all about money. Just as "It takes money to make money" remains a trusted maxim, it's also true that money attracts money (see Tip 9: Sutton, Willie).

Virtue often does go unrewarded. For this reason, the nature of your business will partially determine what your income limit may be. The more money to be found in your industry, the more money you can expect to find its way into your pocket.

You can't control your industry. You can only do combat with your clients. But you can control the most critical factor in the equation—yourself. Only *you* can find the right level for your fees or rates. Experience, along with trial and error, will help. The tips in this chapter will help you to maximize your fees and possibly climb up the fee ladder ahead of schedule.

TIP 43

Size up the whole enchilada.

Determine the total worth of a job and then estimate your fee for the entire job, not as an hourly rate.

Every time I meet with a potential new client, I'm asked the same question. "Do you charge by the hour or by the project?" And every time my response is identical: "Should you steal from me, or should I steal from you?"

With rare exceptions, I charge by the project. That's because copywriting is a creative business. People pay me for ideas and follow-through that are highly subjective in nature. It follows, then, that it can be very difficult to predict exactly how long it will take to come up with the right ideas or concepts, then make them work on a practical level. If your work entails a creative approach—and by that I mean problem-solving as opposed to performing more mechanical functions based on your physical availability—consider that billing by the hour can lead to two unpleasant possibilities:

- You develop an idea in a flash of brilliant insight based on your great talent and years of experience. But you can only bill for an hour or two even though your client would be willing to pay far more for the *value* of your idea. In fact, a less experienced person might charge a lower hourly rate but take many more hours to complete the job—and still fall short of providing your level of quality. Then, to make matters worse, your inept competitor will submit a higher bill. If you charge by the hour you are, in effect, stealing from yourself.
- You approach your task in a leisurely manner to pad your hours, or you do a halfhearted job requiring constant revision. In this case, you are stealing from your client.

What's more, most clients want estimates and will ask you how many hours you think you'll spend on the task and how much you charge an hour. Since your clients cannot control the number of hours it will take you to do the job, they are really asking, "What is your fee?" So it only stands to reason that you should charge by the project.

How do you arrive at a reasonable fee? While Tips 43 to 45 discuss some of the more challenging aspects of fee setting (some jobs have a fairly established worth in and of themselves no matter how many hours you spend on them), the basic formula is simple and obvious: Rate × Hours = Fee.

But what should your rate be? When I started freelancing in 1979, I determined that any job I did had to bring me at least $25 an hour. Of course, I could charge $500 for a job that took ten hours and make a handsome $50 an hour. But again, I was being paid not for my time but for the value of my ideas. What do you need to do to make this formula work for you?

Establish your minimum hourly rate. Although freelancing demands flexibility, you should make this one of the few guidelines you set in concrete—a financial return you will not lower under virtually any circumstances.

Establish your minimum daily and weekly rates. In my early years clients occasionally asked me to work in their offices by the day. I no longer do that except for occasional consulting jobs requiring me to review a client's work or conduct workshops for its staff. For many freelancers, however, work outside their own office (I'm not addressing long-term contract workers here) represents a large portion or perhaps even a majority of their billings. You may wish to discount your hourly rate when a client offers eight hours of work in a day, several days of work in a week, or several weeks of work in a month. But bear in mind that once you're in a client's office, it's hard to get work done for other clients. Furthermore, you may be investing considerable commuting time and expense to get to your daily or weekly job. You must keep your rates consistent with your financial goals. Once you've set your daily and weekly rates, stick to them (see Tip 34).

Determine all the factors that will be reflected in the time you spend working. Factor in research, at home or elsewhere, and travel.

Estimate the time it will take you to do the job correctly. Your reputation, and thus your business, depends on delivering the highest quality work in a timely manner. Be sure you have the time to actually think and weigh ideas.

Add nonroutine out-of-pocket costs to your estimate. I consider one or two FedEx packages or a reference book to be a normal expense for a job. But I generally add to my fees any rush messenger charges necessitated by my client's poor scheduling (not my lack of timeliness) as well as any purchases requested by my client.

Speak with your client immediately if the guidelines within which you are working suddenly change. Don't wait until after you've finished the job (see Tip 33). By then your client may feel it's too late to bring the matter up. And don't simply increase your bill (see Tip 29). If you do that, you'll develop a well-earned and regrettable reputation for a lack of trustworthiness.

I did mention that I occasionally charge by the hour. While these jobs are relatively few, they include certain mechanical tasks for which it might be difficult to estimate a flat fee. I might be asked, for example, to edit a client's presentation into something more workable. I'll gladly do this by the hour. But first I ask my client about the maximum his budget will allow. Then, if I'm in the middle of the job and anticipate I might need more time, I'll call. At this point, my client's decision to increase the budget or cut off work at the established limit is fairly simple, and no feathers get ruffled. Yet even this kind of situation calls for a set estimate. In effect, I'm willing to get *only* my hourly minimum—the floor beneath which I won't go—for the job instead of my usually higher fee.

Value your contribution, your integrity, and your client's need for reliability, and you'll increase your value in the marketplace.

TIP 44

Grid your fees.

Set a top-down sliding scale for large, middle-size, and small clients to ensure fairness for everyone, including yourself.

After my father, Morris, graduated (class of 1921) from the old De Witt Clinton High School in New York City, my grandfather, Samuel, sent him down to the Lower East Side to buy an overcoat. Since my father would be entering the business world (he attended the New York University School of Business at night for eleven years to earn his B.S.), he would need to dress appropriately. The Lower East Side, by far the largest Jewish community in America, had retained much of what its residents and shopkeepers had brought from Eastern Europe. That included haggling.

My father, however—born in Warsaw but brought up in various Manhattan neighborhoods, including Harlem—hated to haggle. By his own account, he went into a shop on Allen Street—an enterprising salesclerk no doubt having whisked him in off the sidewalk—found an overcoat he liked, and asked how much it was. The salesclerk, delighted to deal with a probably inexperienced young man, responded with an inflated price of $22. "I'll give you twenty," my father shot back, and that was that. He doubtless overpaid by at least $8. But to him, the value of the overcoat included avoiding bargaining.

The value of a job is no less different. Fees are negotiated and ultimately settled upon based on the points of view of the involved parties. In short, $2,500 fees for identical jobs may be seen as quite reasonable—indeed, as a bargain—by a large client and as simply not affordable by a small one. Set your fees in stone, and you risk underpricing your work with big clients and overpricing it with small ones. Set single-tier fees too high, and you could lose the small-client market altogether. But if you set your fees too low, you may actually underprice yourself out of the big-client market, since your low fees will arouse suspicion that you are not capable of doing the job at the level they are seeking.

The solution is simple. Following the lead of social service agencies, which establish fees on a sliding scale based on ability to pay, develop a grid *from the top down.* Set fees for each of at least three classifications—corporate, middle-size, and small firms.

Establishing your grid from the top down is a matter of ethics. Set your standard fee at the lowest end of the scale, and you define your worth there. Quote higher fees to large clients, and you are, in effect, allowing yourself to gouge them. But establish what you believe to be your real value at the high end, and you create a baseline enabling you to lower your fees for mid-size and small clients, acknowledging their budget limitations.

Part of my grid might look like this:

Client	*8-page brochure*	*Full-page magazine ad*	*Self-mailer*
Large	$3,000.00	$2,500.00	$3,500.00
Medium	2,500.00	2,000.00	3,000.00
Small	1,750.00	1,500.00	2,500.00

Similarly, I scale my fees for radio commercials based not only on the size of the client but on whether the commercials will be aired nationally, regionally, or locally. This reflects the client's media expenditure and total project budget and helps to determine the give-and-take involved in arriving at a just fee. It bears repeating, however, that your basic fees should always start at the top and be discounted to smaller clients or when smaller budgets are involved.

Just as important, avoid those indelicate pauses when a client's question about your fees leaves you pondering the question. Set your grid *in writing, in advance.* If you can't remember your fee for a particular job and client size, feel free to say that you have to check your fee schedule. You'll not only maximize your income over the long term but avoid appearing to have no knowledge of your own worth. Successful negotiations and enduring relationships develop from positions of confidence and professionalism.

And what if a client offers a fee that's *higher* than the one you've written into your grid? Accept it gracefully and without comment; then use it as the baseline in your relationship with that client. Remember, value, like beauty, is in the eye of the beholder. Fees for the same type of job can vary as greatly as prices in a Third World marketplace. If, later, that client should ask you to agree to a lower fee on another project based on budget restrictions, you can return the good faith you've been shown.

Structure your fee grid, use it as the basis of negotiations, then review it periodically (see Tip 45) in order to establish the structure for a thriving freelance business.

TIP 45

Reach for the moon.

Conduct an annual review to determine whether your fees are consistent with your talent, your experience, and the marketplace. And give yourself raises.

When I started freelancing, I had no real idea of my worth. I had set a goal for my income (see Tip 34) but had no concrete guidelines. Over time, my work with a variety of clients enabled me to get a better handle on the market. And the longer I freelanced the more confident I became. This enabled me to translate my increasing experience into added value and periodically grant myself modest fee increases across my grid (see Tip 44).

I was fairly satisfied with my fees until a *client* with whom I'd worked closely for many years reviewed my estimate for a project and uttered three words that caused my income to soar: "That's not enough."

The fact is, I had not been totally in tune with the marketplace on the highest grid levels. My fees were fairly well under those that large clients were willing to pay—and, of course, more than an order of magnitude below what most agencies charged their clients. I know this because my client, who had been an account supervisor at one of the world's largest direct response advertising agencies, would often tell me about the rather hefty fees his former agency charged for similar jobs. Once my eyes were fully opened, I began to raise my fees substantially.

How often you consider giving yourself a raise is up to you. I recommend that you conduct a review of your fees—just as employers review salaries with their employees—at least once a year. How much of a raise can you give yourself? As a freelancer, your decision will be a highly individual one based on the work you do, the competition, and the size and scope of your market. Here are some guidelines:

Weigh your income versus your goals. Determine whether you are truly satisfied with your income. The best incentive to increase fees is the realization that you are simply not living the life you want to live—and that you exercise a great deal of control over your lifestyle and financial well-being. You *deserve* to earn a good living.

Check out the marketplace. Do as much research as you can. Chat with friends who hire or work with freelancers in your industry. Ask them what they consider to be reasonable fees. Talk with other freelancers to find out how they set their fee structures. Read trade publications or books like *Writer's Market,* which publish typical fees. However, these fees cover a wide range. Your market value may be at the high or low end, above or below that of your competitors, based on your experience, talent, and perceived worth.

Ask yourself which of your upper-end fees were readily accepted—and why. Look over your books to find your best-paying jobs. Then ask yourself why you were able to command such high fees. Was the size of your client a determinant? What about the quality of your client's product or service, your client's general pay scale, the need for your specific talents, and your ability to deliver on a tight schedule? This will help you propose the right fee to each client while profiling the *kinds* of clients you want to work for. Conversely, see which clients and jobs provided fees you believe were too low. Write out a profile of the kinds of clients and jobs that you should not be actively seeking or that you should be *refusing*. Accepting too many low-end projects can pigeonhole you as a low-quality provider and undeservedly keep you from being considered for more lucrative projects. But there's a small catch (see Tip 46).

Stand up for yourself in negotiations. You don't have to be unreasonable to secure fees that meet your objectives. Give-and-take characterizes most negotiations. Of course, there are times when a client is locked into a budget. Giving today may mean taking tomorrow. Blend self-confidence with sensitivity, and you can command larger fees on many of your projects over the long run.

Raise your fees to existing clients in small increments. If you've normally been doing a certain job for $750, consider raising your fee to $900 or $1,000 rather than the $1,500 or $2,000 you suddenly find out you deserve. A shocked client may turn elsewhere even if your proposed new fee is fair. That's because "fair" is whatever enables *both* of you to reach agreement. Small raises are easier for clients to absorb. Additional small raises in the future will keep your income growing, much like the compounding of interest in a savings account or certificate of deposit, which produces meaningful growth over time.

Adjust your grid to the right level for new clients. Charging a below-market fee to existing clients doesn't mean you're locked in when it comes to setting fees for new ones. If $2,000 is the right fee for a specific project and you've never charged that much before, start *now.*

Adjust your grid in writing. Once you've determined what your top fee should be for a particular type of job, enter it into your grid. Then create new fees for the middle- and small-client levels. You need not raise the fees on each level by the same amount or percentage. Just be sure you're consistent and in the ballpark. Print out your revised grid and refer to it whenever you bid on a job.

Raise the level of your jobs. I wrote classified ads for more than one client when I first started. The fees were small, but I needed the work. Would I write classifieds today? No. I need to do larger jobs with larger companies to continue building my freelance business. Most freelancers, when they start out, will take any available job. I did. As your business grows, however, you'll find it's much more profitable to do fewer big jobs than many small ones, Of course, you don't have to increase the quality of your clients all at once, and you can remain loyal to small clients you like. But over time, you should definitely put behind you those clients who can't help you meet your objectives. (For additional comments, see Tip 46.)

Pay as much attention to your fee and income levels as you do to the needs of your clients, who are also in business to grow and profit. Your attentiveness will pay off handsomely.

TIP 46

Stay down to earth.

Stick to your minimum rates and sound guidelines to leverage small jobs into bigger income.

This tip is short and obvious—but not obvious enough to be eliminated from this book. In Tip 45 I mentioned avoiding small, low-fee projects that can pigeonhole you as a low-quality provider and undeservedly keep you from being considered for better-paying projects. There are times, however, when small, low-fee jobs can be great profit builders. You can make the most of those small jobs when the following conditions apply:

The job pays at least your established minimum hourly compensation. While an hourly rate does not represent your best income opportunity, it does provide a basic platform on which to base all your fees. (See Tip 43.)

The fee is comparable to those you've charged for similar small projects. If so, no sacrifice is involved. If not, be aware that underpricing yourself leads to weakening your fee grid and poses the risk of a downward plunge from which you may not be able to extricate yourself.

You are doing the job for a good client who normally asks you to work on larger projects. Even if you've gone to the top in your market, maintaining good client relationships demands that you respond to a client's occasional request for nuts-and-bolts work and a reasonable favor.

You actually have time in your schedule. Never jeopardize a large job you're currently working on or projects you may be expecting to begin. If making a few extra dollars erodes the quality of your work on a more important project, you'll end up losing money when you disappoint a high-paying client and unhinge that relationship. Of course, freelancers are, by definition, hungry businesspeople always looking for work. But grasping at any job that presents itself can keep you too busy to seek and find the kinds of clients and jobs you really want. The saying "I'm too busy working to make money" has been around for a long time! So what if your schedule is tight and a good client needs help? A $25,000-a-year client swings more weight than a $5,000-a-year client. Sleep less.

You trust the client. Small jobs from small clients can create big headaches when it's time to collect your fee. No job is done until you get paid. Know your client. An up-front fee can help prevent a nasty problem (see Tip 49).

The job could go into your portfolio. Work demanding true creativity and problem-solving can never be judged by size and price alone. A small job that will look impressive on your résumé or become a sample with which to lure new clients can be a good investment. The flip side—minimize the amount of showcase work you do to avoid choking off real moneymaking jobs.

There's more than one way to make an impact on your bottom line. Know when to think small and you'll produce bigger results.

TIP 47

Avoid the 800-pound gorilla.

Free yourself from dominance by a single client and from the complacency that can lead to major disaster.

You know the old joke: "Where does an 800-pound gorilla sleep? Anywhere it wants." But the joke could be on you if you let any one client get too large.

I've mentioned several times that my former employer was responsible for 90 percent of my billings during my first full year as a freelancer. I was delighted to have his support. But I also knew that the viability of my business hung by a thread on his willingness to maintain the relationship. If at any time he decided that he no longer liked me or my work—or if he simply became interested in someone who could offer him a different perspective—I'd have had a crisis on my hands. Of course, that would have led to my spending more time on my new-business efforts. But then, I wouldn't have had anything else to do.

Fortunately, the 800-pound gorilla stayed pleased with my work, and we developed an even better relationship as one company owner dealing with another rather than as employer and employee (see Tip 5). Best of all, I began to attract new clients just as my ex-boss hired a solid pro to take over my old position and had fewer reasons to call on me.

Does a single client who keeps you moderately busy really present a danger? Absolutely! The 800-pound gorilla can begin dictating your fees rather than negotiating them. When you're locked into a restrictive relationship, the gorilla has all the clout. Worse, the gorilla can keep you just busy enough to make it difficult for you to seek new clients. Your dependency grows. And as it does, your income remains subdued and flat.

"But," you counter, "what if that gorilla is very generous? Perhaps even a small gold mine?" No question, you'll do well. For a while. But even the richest gold mines eventually peter out. Gold mines can suddenly start losing business, cut budgets, acquire new partners, sell their companies, or become intrigued with one of your competitors . . .

Good friends of mine—a married couple—own a small advertising agency and staff it with one additional employee. I frequently work on projects with them. For several years the vast majority of their billings came from a mutual fund company with which I had no involvement. That client kept them extremely busy, agreed to attractive fees, and paid its bills on time. Doing well, my friends were able to buy a house, make some renovations, and take trips to Hawaii, New York, and Italy. Then their client merged with another company and announced its intention to shift all of its advertising to the Midwest.

Fortunately, my friends had several months to begin their adjustment. They also had a foot in the door with a high-tech company for whom they did occasional projects, although this new client could not in any way replace the one they soon lost. As I write, they are building a sound relationship with their high-tech client to gain a larger share of the client's workload. Furthermore, one employee of this high-tech company left and will doubtless call on them in her new job. Hopefully, one client will become two. But the emotional and financial shock, though not fatal, has hurt.

How can you keep an 800-pound gorilla from crushing your business?

Keep track of your individual client billings and check them regularly. A running account of your client-by-client billings will enable you to see how you're doing at a glance. Before one client remotely begins to dominate your billings, sound the alarm, shake yourself awake, and . . .

Accelerate your search for new business. Complacency is the worst enemy of any business. No matter how busy you are, you must maintain good relationships with existing clients if you want to keep their business, and you must establish new contacts with prospects. When a gorilla looms in the mist, your new business efforts become even more important.

Leverage your best work to show prospects. Money is never enough. In order to obtain new clients, you have to produce work of which you can be proud. One of the best ways to expand your client base is to make sure that you have enough successes in your portfolio—and that you continually enhance your portfolio. When necessary, flex your muscles and push that gorilla to let you do your best.

Put money away. This advice pops up throughout this book, and for good reason. When your gorilla turns away from you, your income can virtually disappear within a month. The greater your reliance on a single client, the heftier your reserve funds will need to be.

Spread your business around to a number of clients, and you'll maintain a healthy spreadsheet year after year.

Chapter 7

BILLING AND COLLECTING

When I was a very young boy growing up in Queens, one of New York City's five boroughs, the Yankees appeared in virtually every World Series. I loved early autumn because I was a rabid Yankees fan. I also loved my aunt Anne and uncle Moe, my second parents, who lived in Brooklyn and were ardent Dodger fans. But I was not averse to winning easy money from them.

Every fall, Uncle Moe and I would bet on the Series. I would take the Yankees; Uncle Moe would take the Dodgers or any other National League team. Regrettably, Uncle Moe died before the Dodgers captured their first championship in 1955, beating the Yankees in seven games. Until that time, I won a lot of money. And, of course, I never had trouble collecting. Uncle Moe paid his debts.

Business situations can be just as exciting but not necessarily as certain. You win a new client, do the job well, receive praise, and send out your invoice. But you don't complete the cycle—and achieve the success for which you've striven—until you receive a check for the full amount. And it clears.

I find the task of sending out invoices to be somewhat euphoric. Often, receiving payment doesn't match that emotional high. But having to act when payment hasn't been received definitely is the lowest part of my day.

How you structure your billing and collecting procedures will ultimately determine the viability of your freelance business. Everything before and after this chapter only leads up or cycles around to the moment when you actually get paid.

Never leave billing and collecting to chance. The following tips will explain why—and guide you in maximizing your cash flow while minimizing headaches, potential and real.

TIP 48

Lock in all you can.

Set up retainers to provide guaranteed income and scheduled payments you can rely on month after month.

Some years back, before the World Wide Web gained great popularity, an ad agency client of mine asked me to edit a local newspaper's movie reviews each week. These brief blurbs appeared on an interactive information system displayed around San Francisco. The job was small, as was the fee, but it extended over a period of six months or so. When I mentioned my $200 monthly fee to an associate, she expressed her envy. "But it's not very much money," I protested. She retorted, "But at least it's something you can count on every month."

Retainers may not always be lucrative, for reasons I'll soon explain, but they definitely provide income you can count on—a minimum on which to build the rest of your monthly fees. There are, however, two key tricks involved in taking advantage of retainer income. First, you have to find a client who's willing to make the deal. And, second, you have to structure the deal correctly.

There are good reasons why a client may be hesitant to offer you a retainer. A client who is obligated to pay you a fixed fee may feel unsure that all of your paid-up time will be used. Clients do like to get their money's worth. Your client may also believe that she's giving up her options—that she must depend on you to be good at everything that needs to be done rather than choosing the right individual for each specific task.

You can counter your client's doubts with two good arguments. First, a retainer enables a client to budget efficiently. Your client knows just what will be spent on your services each month. And second, your client may be able to obtain your services for less because you can charge less per hour in return for a guaranteed number of hours of work. Call it a volume discount, if you like—it could be enough to enable you to keep a client you might otherwise lose.

What's more, you can offer your client exclusive rights to you, denying the client's competition your services. This represents an additional strategy—one which requires that you be at the top of your field, however—and demands a retainer large enough to compensate you for the opportunities you are willing to forgo.

There's a flip side to the business of retainers, of course. In return for a guaranteed monthly income, you will have to give up work on a project basis, which is generally more profitable. I've found through experience that a retainer can actually lower a client's billings over the course of a year. (I agreed to the retainer because the client told me that all her service suppliers would be on retainer—to fix costs—or not work for her at all.)

After weighing all the options, you may decide to go on retainer when you can. The right agreement can be fair to both sides and be very reassuring when your other clients slide away during a downward cycle. Here's what you need to do:

Determine the amount of time your client is buying each month. Clients may mistakenly see a retainer as open-ended, entitling them to all of your time. That's definitely a skewed vision! Imagine agreeing to a retainer that would pay you a quarter of your monthly billings goal, then spending 80 percent of your time for it. Like the 800-pound gorilla (see Tip 47), the open-ended retainer can crush you at a whim.

Agree on an hourly rate to determine your total retainer fee. If your regular hourly minimum charge is $60, and your client would like to buy twenty hours of your time each month, you might be willing to structure your retainer rate at $50 an hour. Your monthly retainer will be 20 hours × $50 = $1,000. (For more on hourly fees, see Tip 43.)

Settle on your rate for additional hours. Since retainers are *not* open-ended, you also need to agree on a rate you'll charge for every hour over the agreed limit. You might wangle the same $50, since you've already discounted your rate. Or, to encourage more business, you might offer $45 an hour for everything over your twenty monthly hours. The more your client relies on you, the more your client saves.

Fix fail-safe minimum hours. What if you work fewer than your established twenty hours in a month? You still get paid in full—the number of hours you work is your client's responsibility—unless you agree to some other arrangement. You may decide, for example, that if you work fewer than fifteen hours in a month, you must still be paid for fifteen hours rather than the full twenty. Work more than fifteen hours, and you must be paid for the full twenty. This is a subject for negotiation—one that can help a client to see your retainer as a smart business decision and that can protect you from arbitrary decisions.

Set the date on which you will be paid in full. Your client now has a fixed expense. There should be no question about a fixed date on which you will receive your check. Mail or fax your invoice at the end of the last day of the month or on the first of the following month and let your client know if you do not receive your payment on the agreed due date.

Put your agreement in writing. I remember a short sentence printed on the memo pads of a retail client when I was an ad agency employee in Texas: "Verbal instructions don't go." How true! No matter how wonderful your client, only a detailed written agreement, signed and dated, can protect your best interests. It must include *everything* decided on by you and your client, including all the details discussed above plus the *length* of the agreement. You may wish to suggest trying the retainer for three months with each party retaining an option to renew or renegotiate for another three months. You may also agree to a thirty-day cancellation notice, which will provide you with a final month of work prior to terminating an agreement before it's finished. This can keep both you and your client comfortable if your retainer agreement extends to six months and more.

Track your hours daily. Your retainer pays you against a fixed number of hours. You cannot give those hours away. Keep a log—electronic or paper—something like this:

Date	*Time*	*Task*	*Hours*	*Total*
4/13	9–9:30A	Century brochure	0.50	0.50
4/13	2–4:30P	Press release	2.50	3.00
4/15	10–11:30A	Century brochure	1.50	4.50
4/16	1–3:15P	Annual report letter	2.25	6.75
			Weekly total	6.75
			Month to date	12.50

Keep your client up to date. Fax or E-mail your hours at the end of each week, then at the end of the month. (Not unimportantly, your weekly reports will also help your client assign your hours to multiple cost centers when applicable.) If it appears that you'll reach your set number of hours earlier in the month than expected, notify your client so she can either adjust your workload or budget for additional hours. And *always* notify your client *before* you go into overtime.

One retainer can be quite a comfort. Two or three can put your business on very sound footing. Reach the right agreement, and you'll reach—or surpass—the $100,000 level much sooner.

TIP 49

Fix the numbers up front.

Provide a detailed written estimate to fully explain what you'll be doing and how much your services will cost. Then get it signed before you start working.

Ever since I've known her—and that goes back over half a century now—my mother, Blanche, has never looked at a price tag. Her philosophy of shopping has always been simple: "If I want it, I buy it. And your father pays." It worked. My mother saw. She bought. And right up to the end of his life, my father paid gladly. In fact, when my mother paid cash, she asked my father not only for that sum back but for additional cash as well. He complied. I've never figured out the logic of their arrangement, but I do know that my father was delighted to be able to provide generously for his family (he also made an unusually large number of interest-free, no-questions-asked loans to family members). My mother saw her primary job as keeping him happy.

Your clients, of course, shop for services differently. Their superiors don't share my parents' "hang the cost" philosophy. Clients want to know the price in advance, and they should. An estimate enables your client to budget accurately. Nothing is more disastrous than beginning work on a project only to find that there's not enough money to pay for it. An estimate also protects *you* against clients who decide, illogically but all too commonly, that your fee is simply too large—*after* you've satisfactorily completed the task.

There's no great trick to making estimates work for you. Here's what you need to do:

Create an estimate form. Since each freelancer's business is unique, you'll need to develop an estimate form that meets your individual requirements. But don't fret. Estimates tend to be basic. Stumped? If you're still an employee, check your company's own estimate forms and those of freelancers who work for the firm. If you're already freelancing, ask a former employer if you can review his estimate forms. The following suggestions, however, should guide you clearly. Then experience will lead you to modify your estimate forms as needed.

Include your job number, a project description, and the date. Estimate forms serve as handy reference materials only when they are complete. (See Tip 18 for related ideas on keeping control of your business procedures.)

Determine your fee and expenses in detail. Take the time to get an accurate picture of what's expected of you. Breaking down your fee and your expenses, if any, can help you get a real handle on exactly what you'll have to do and how much you'll spend to complete a project. An extra plus—it can also justify the cost of the project to your client who may not realize all that's involved. Of course, if nothing else is involved, an estimate can be as simple as one line describing the service, noting the completion date, and specifying the fee—"Writing 8-page brochure by September 15, $2,000." Remember, however, that your estimate is your word (see Tip 29).

Add a contingency when appropriate. Few jobs of any size escape unanticipated client changes. You may wish to add a 10 percent contingency to help you avoid wrangling with your client when you bill and to allow your client to budget sufficiently up front and avoid going to his superior or into his budget for unanticipated funds.

Include sales tax when applicable. If you provide a tangible product, show appropriate sales tax as a subcategory. Don't assume your client will figure sales tax into his budget. Do realize that your client must be able to differentiate between your fee and the projected invoice total, so you won't appear to be padding your fee. I've worked with designers and photographers who failed to include sales tax in their estimates, then had clients complain that their bills were higher than their estimates—and refuse to pay anything but the estimated amount. To a client, the bottom line *is* the bottom line.

Include time frames. Your estimate should include a project completion date, but you will also need to provide your client with information on when you'll finish *each stage* leading to completion. If you want to submit a separate project schedule, that's fine. But create a schedule at the same time you prepare your estimate (you can include the number of workdays for each stage rather than specific dates if the deadline is up in the air) to give yourself a structure within which to work. Then obtain prompt client response as each stage is completed and submitted, and make sure you know you can get the work done.

Keep a copy for reference. This may seem too obvious to mention, but believe me, any agreement that's not in your files can lead to disaster.

Get every estimate signed before you start. Submitting an estimate does not equate to securing a client's approval. Yes, you may accept a good client's oral agreement over the phone—although you have the right to make it your standard business practice to get every estimate signed. On the other hand, *never* accept an oral okay from a first-time client, one about whom you have any suspicions, or who has a history of late payment. (To learn more about protecting yourself, see Tip 50.)

Make your fees and expenses clear up front, and you'll gain a clear advantage by eliminating arguments when you submit your bills.

TIP 50

Be an early bird.

Bill in advance whenever possible, and require a deposit to separate serious new clients from "tire kickers."

Every once in a while I hear a fellow freelancer utter the five most disturbing words imaginable in reference to billing their clients: "I'll get around to it." I much prefer the five words an associate of mine frequently counsels: "Bill early and bill often." That advice is sound. While it seems obvious that you can bill only once for a completed job, that's not exactly so. And you always have the option to send invoices sooner rather than later—*much* sooner if you do it right. In practice, this philosophy can turn your cash flow from an eerie drip-drip-drip into a raging waterfall. Result? You're able to pay your bills on time and maintain your reputation as an upstanding businessperson.

A seminar I attended some years ago (see Tip 42) provided me with a sound basis for keeping my own cash flow streaming smoothly. The speaker's wisdom: "Bill on estimate."

Many advertising agencies bill on estimate. Companies in other industries surely do the same. Their invoices go out as soon as their estimates have been approved so that they can receive payment, in whole or in part, to cover not only their fees but their out-of-pocket expenses as well. Because copywriting is my freelance core skill, I have few out-of-pocket expenses, and they are usually minor. But I do have a mortgage to pay along with grocery bills, life insurance, health insurance, and all the other costs of contemporary life.

You can avoid delayed payments from some clients by doing the following:

Bill on estimate when you have considerable out-of-pocket expenses. Whether you're a marketing consultant hiring a designer to create a brochure, a designer purchasing stock photography, a paralegal bringing someone in to transcribe an interview on cassette, a public relations expert hiring a media consultant, or a programmer subcontracting code development, you've taken on a major expense for which you are responsible. Negotiate with your client to bill your total out-of-pocket expenses—and possibly part of your fee as well—up front. This way you'll be able to pay your own bills on time and you'll avoid getting harrying calls from your contractors and suppliers, who also have bills to pay.

Bill when you've completed the first phase of your project prior to client revisions. Whether you're charging a project fee or an hourly rate, this can save you weeks or even months of headaches. Some clients, regardless of the schedules to which they've agreed, take a surprisingly leisurely approach to reviewing the initial work presented to them. You can't let their lack of a timely response stand in the way of your cash flow. Will you be taking advantage of your clients? Not at all. Remember, at this stage, you've invested considerable time and effort and not seen a dime. Also, advise your clients that even if they're still reviewing your work when you get your check, you'll complete any and all work that's routine to the assignment. A good client will put your invoice through right away.

Bill in phases. Some clients may not accept an invoice for your full fee on estimate or at any time prior to completion of the job. You can still speed cash flow effectively by billing progressively. Divide your estimate into two phases—one for preliminary work like a first draft, comprehensive layout, or prototype; and a second one for completion. You can even break a job down into three or more phases. If you're charging an hourly rate, arrange to bill every week or two, and certainly no less often than once a month.

Bill part or all of your fee up front if you're not comfortable with a client. Even when a new client comes from a referral, you are taking someone else's word that your prospect is accountable and will pay on time—or pay at all. When individuals or small companies call you, the odds go up that they may not be totally serious or trustworthy. Or you may meet with a client whose attitude or business environment seems questionable. If you hear a new client yell at employees, your warning light should flash immediately. If a client's office is shabby or his attitude is unpleasant, get ready for trouble. Good intentions and poor credit risks often go hand in hand. Your best response? If you actually stay to hear what this client has to say, make *partial or full payment in advance* a nonnegotiable condition for accepting the job. New clients willing to make an advance partial payment virtually always pay the balance on time. I can't tell you much about suspect clients who refuse to pay part of an estimate in advance, because I haven't any. I walk away from them immediately.

However you handle advance billing—and you'll have to do it on a case-by-case basis—be sure that you at least cover your out-of-pocket expenses. If anyone gets burned, it should be you, not your suppliers and subcontractors (see Tip 57).

Bill in advance as often as you can, and you'll advance your financial well-being considerably.

TIP 51

Get your timing down.

Put your regular billing on a schedule and keep to it.

If you're the parent of a teenager, you know that teens understand higher mathematics better than they let on. For example, teens easily comprehend the concept of infinity. That's the amount of money they believe you have available to spend on their needs. They understand Einstein's theory of relativity, too, particularly as it relates to time slowing down and speeding up. Ask a teen to clean her room, and time extends forever, moving in slower-than-slow motion. On the other hand, tell a teen that you've just returned from the supermarket with soda, chips, and ice cream, and your sparkling kitchen becomes a mess in something akin to a nanosecond.

It's tempting to take a similarly relative view when it comes to billing. Getting detailed paperwork completed and mailed is a chore that some freelancers allow to stretch on and on. Yet everyone wants to get paid in no time at all. Even if you consider billing to be tedium, you have to generate invoices to generate income. You can't always bill early (see Tip 50), but you *can* always bill on time. And you should. To do it, consider taking these steps:

Keep all the bills you receive from suppliers and contractors in a dedicated job file. When billing day comes, all your paperwork will be right at your fingertips. You'll get your invoices out on time and save time doing it.

Bill as soon as the job is complete whether or not cash flow is a problem. Put your invoice together as soon as your client gives you the okay—and mail it the same day. It's better to take a few minutes away from other business than to suffer each day the mail carrier fails to bring a check.

Call suppliers and contractors immediately to ask for their billing totals. Just because someone else is casual about getting paid doesn't mean that you should be. If you've just completed a job but you don't know what your out-of-pocket costs are, ring your suppliers and get the figures by fax so that you'll have written backup when your invoices come.

Establish a regular billing day, and bill weekly if possible. I usually bill on Fridays. And I never skip a Friday if a job is complete. Waiting longer—for example, saving billing for the last day of the month—will mean a delay in receiving money your client owes you. Remember, there is nothing wrong with asking a client to keep her end of the bargain. It's not rude to bill immediately. It's smart.

Don't go more than two weeks without billing. You finish a job on Tuesday. Wednesday is hectic. Thursday you put out one fire after another. And Friday is a zoo—no time for billing. So? Do it Monday. Do it Tuesday if you must. But don't let a second week go by without getting your invoice out. Given some clients' casual handling of invoices (see Rooms, Cleaning by Teenagers, above), you could find yourself in a difficult situation when your rent, phone, and supplier bills come due.

Review your job files weekly (see Tip 18) to make sure no job has gone unbilled. Don't simply assume that your billing is up to date. Keep accurate job records that include the date your invoice was sent. Then check those records each week on your billing day—even when you have no bills to get out—to pick up any job you may have overlooked.

If this tip seems to read long, remember, the number of words is relative. Given the importance of timely billing, the extra few seconds you've just spent reading this advice could save you hours of regret.

Create a sound routine for billing, and you'll make getting paid quickly routine as well.

TIP 52

Play Scrooge in reverse.

Notify your clients of changes before you send invoices. Bill accurately and in detail. And always treat a client's financial interests with respect.

Considering my freelance experiences with a certain type of professional, I should not like my niece's husband, Michael. In spite of the fact that he is the father of my grandnephew, Matthew, and fits perfectly into our family (he's a bigger sports nut than I ever was), Michael's former business role sends shudders up the spines of advertising people like me. He was a compliance officer for a bank. Michael, who's also an attorney, was responsible for making sure that everything his bank did or said met federal and state regulations.

Why should this be a problem for a copywriter? I have done work for a lot of financial institutions and insurance companies, and many lawyers in Michael's former position, attempting to protect their companies from liability, not only render legal opinions but change copy often—and often grotesquely. "Legal said you have to say it this way" is a sentence commonly heard by both freelancers and employees in most industries.

However, an important lesson learned years ago has buffered my reaction to attorneys' changes, no matter how strongly I may disagree with them. A former boss once explained that, like it or not, financial institutions handle other people's money. They *have* to be—or at least they have to *appear* to be—circumspect in everything they do, given the savings and loan scandals of the 1980s. I've always taken that to heart.

That advice should be reflected in your own client relationships. You are obligated to respect your clients fully, and that includes understanding that their money is not yours for the asking. Therefore, you are also obligated to make sure that your billing processes and invoices meet several key standards that will ultimately protect your own interests:

Notify your client* in advance *when you believe an increase in your fee is justified. It's not uncommon for a client to change the direction or parameters of a project once you've begun and after you have invested considerable time and effort—and possibly expense. As a result, increasing your fee for doing more work is only logical and fair. But don't anticipate that your client understands this. And don't wait to surprise your client with the fee increase on your invoice. Call, fax, or E-mail the client as soon as it becomes apparent that you will have to increase your fee. Then reissue a detailed estimate explaining your increase in writing—and get it acknowledged.

Explain added charges in your invoice, even after issuing a new estimate. Clients—both your contacts and the folks in accounting—often compare estimates and invoices prior to authorizing payment. They want to compare apples to apples, and justifiably so. All your charges should be clearly detailed. This will help you avoid problems in two ways. First, you'll keep your client from calling you to say your bill is incomplete, unclear, or in error. That kind of call always puts you on the defensive. Even when you're right, you may end up losing some of your client's confidence. Second, you'll have a written record to refer to when a similar job comes up and questions arise about your new estimate and the items for which you will be charging. A verified cost history can avoid unnecessary discussions.

Keep everything in writing. It bears repeating that with many clients, oral okays are not sufficient. Even your best clients may respond to pressure from challenging business situations and haranguing bosses by questioning your honest communications concerning fees and expenses, whether they reflect changes on an invoice or your original estimate. A written record provides you with the proof you need to support your position and avoid blowups over who said what and when.

Be clear about the payments you are due, and you'll clearly demonstrate your professionalism and worth to your clients.

TIP 53

Utilize the strategic retreat.

Lower your estimates when you realize that substantially less work will be required and discount your bills when less work was actually performed.

In May and June of 1940, a year and a half before the United States entered World War II, the British and French fought the

Germans in northern France. Unfortunately they were soundly defeated and forced to retreat by boat from the Continent. But the Battle of Dunkirk came to represent a victory within a horrible defeat—the heroic evacuation of 350,000 troops, who would later return to France during the D day invasion of June 6, 1944.

The strategic retreat is not just a standard military maneuver. There are times when freelancers, like all other businesspeople, must give ground and agree to reduce their fees before an estimate is signed—or even after a job has been undertaken or completed. If you yield voluntarily—and better yet, proactively—what you give up will often be repaid to you over and again. We know who won at Normandy.

A reduction may be not only necessary but advisable in some situations:

When your estimate conflicts with your client's budget. A good client will have an impact on your income not just this week or this month but over the long term. As a result, not every project needs to be wildly profitable. While no client has the right to expect you to work for free or at cost, any good client should believe that you will lower your margin when a budget is tight. If you sense that your normal fee presents a difficulty, reduce it without waiting for your client to ask. Good clients will frequently find extra dollars on succeeding jobs to repay you. Even when they don't, the soundness of your long-term relationship will keep your business profitable and growing.

When you overestimated the work you had to do. There are times when a job can't be clearly defined, and you still have to submit an estimate for a fixed fee. Afterward you find that your fee is far higher than that which the work mandated. While wildly profitable jobs are exhilarating, you can make a wise investment by billing less and notifying your client that you're doing so. You can decrease your fee by a modest amount and still make a good profit. Even better, you can demonstrate good faith and integrity—one of the best ways to build a truly strong relationship with any client. What's more, decreasing your fee in such situations sets a sound example for your client when the reverse occurs and you do *more* work than anticipated and request a larger fee (see Tip 52). Fairness is a two-way street.

When your client overestimated the work required. This corollary to the above is simple. Your client gives you a job and agrees to your estimate. As time goes by, the job is scaled down, or it becomes apparent that less effort will be required of you than you originally believed necessary. You send an invoice for the fee you originally estimated. Your client calls and asks you to lower your fee. You take a deep breath, think briefly about what you could have done with the extra money, then say, "You're right. Let's talk about what fee would be suitable." You can, of course, insist that your client's signature on your estimate remains the final word. Unfortunately, "Don't bother calling" will be your client's final word.

Lower your fees judiciously, and you can raise your income substantially.

TIP 54

Study the calendar.

Establish reasonable periods within which you expect to be paid. Then track your outstanding invoices to find out whether you're being paid on time.

Back in the early 1970s, when I was a young and inexperienced copywriter at an ad agency in San Antonio, I got an opportunity to pick up some experience in a hurry. We were pitching an established local furniture and appliance retailer that was about to open a warehouse-showroom—a fairly new concept at the time.

The presentation went well until, after we had established our credentials and creative expertise, the subject of billing came up. The client mentioned, without apology, that he didn't pay his bills for at least ninety days and then only when asked. He would hold on to our money as long as he could.

The agency principals said nothing. I sat stone-faced but stunned, not only at the client's statement but at my bosses' silence. If I'd had the authority to do so, I would have replied, "Our policy is thirty days. I hope you can work with that or something close to it. If not, thank you for inviting us to discuss your account. And good-bye."

Looking back, I find that my stance remains absolutely unchanged. The agency opened itself up to a real nightmare, and I don't doubt that my bosses—nice men for whom I felt great affection—paid for it in more ways than one. We did get the account, and the client was not pleasant to deal with. One example bothered me greatly: We proposed a television commercial for recliners featuring a professional basketball player with the San Antonio Spurs, who had moved from Dallas. The client's brother-in-law, who also served as the client's advertising manager, turned down our proposal. He said that the Spurs and pro basketball would never make it. Wrong! The Spurs became highly successful and one of four American Basketball Association franchises to merge into the NBA a few years later. But at least I got to have lunch with one of the team's stars.

What lesson should every freelancer learn from this? It often takes *two* to pile up overdue invoices. Unfortunately, all of us will come up with a bad apple from time to time. But you definitely can minimize your risk. Here's how:

Speak with your clients about a mutually agreeable payment cycle. My standard requirement is net thirty—I expect to be paid in full within thirty days of my invoice date. But I also know that clients pay their bills in different ways. For example, one client pays on the fourth Friday after receiving a bill. Since we are in the same suite of offices and the Postal Service does not factor in, I know the exact date on which I'll get my check. Another outstanding client pays thirty days from my invoice date. Every time. If a check doesn't arrive in thirty days—a rarity—I realize that the invoice probably got misplaced. I wait a week, then call. They send a check the next day. A major computer manufacturer for whom I work pays in thirty-five days. But some of my clients are scattered around the country and often have to receive my invoices, then send them to another city. I might wait forty or forty-five days, but the checks always come. One agency client of mine finds it difficult to pay in thirty days, so we've agreed on forty-five days. The system works. Friends who run a much smaller agency must wait until they get paid by their clients before they can pay me. Their integrity is unquestioned, and I have a personal interest in their well-being, so my invoices to them are due whenever they have the funds. Payment always arrives in less than sixty days.

Make your due dates reasonable. You must work with your clients' business procedures to avoid tensions and misunderstandings. But you have a right to expect your clients to meet *your* needs as well. When a client needs a little extra time to pay, you can work with that—as long as the client always keeps his word. When a client wants an extended period prior to payment—sixty days or more—you have a potential crisis on your hands. A client who can't or won't pay bills within a reasonable time frame either represents a poor credit risk or simply refuses to value you as a business associate. Unless you can work out partial payment or a reasonable payment schedule, sever the relationship. Sooner or later you'll get burned.

Send the bill to the right person. Some clients want invoices to go directly to their accounting departments. Others want project managers to see them first, okay them, then pass them on. This may affect a client's ability to pay in thirty days, particularly if your key contact leaves town—and leaves your invoice in a pile of papers. But you can overcome that obstacle. . . .

Fax a bill when that's acceptable. When cash flow becomes a real problem, mailing your invoice could cause a delay of several days, particularly during the holidays in December. Find out if your client accepts faxed invoices and, if so, whether you should follow up with a mailed original. Further, when you know that your client is going on vacation or out of town on business, you can always ask that you be allowed to fax your invoice for immediate processing.

Be sure your invoice contains all the information your client requires. Find out if a job number and purchase order number are required. Get that information *in advance*, and include the number on your bill along with your own invoice number, job description, date of invoice, and terms.

Consider offering discounts to get tardy clients moving. Manufacturers and wholesalers do this all the time. You can make a discount standard or offer one just to slow-paying clients who might respond to the savings. For example, your terms can be "2 percent net 10, full payment net 30," which means the client can take 2 percent off your invoice if you receive payment in ten days but must pay in full after that with the balance due in thirty days. What discount terms you offer, and to whom, are up to you.

Inform your clients when you have special needs. Many clients are surprisingly flexible. If your invoice carries considerable out-of-pocket costs, your client may agree to speed up the payment cycle so you can cover those expenses. Bear in mind, however, that net thirty is the general standard in business, and your clients may not accede to any term that's shorter. Further, you can be treated with the respect due a full-fledged business only if you demonstrate financial stability. It's your responsibility to have sufficient resources to pay your bills on time. Panic fails to instill confidence.

Each weekly billing day, check to see which invoices are overdue. (See Tips 54–57 for handling this problem.) Never assume that your check will arrive on time. On the other hand, don't get nervous on day thirty or thirty-one. Remember, a client has to receive your bill, which can take several days to arrive by mail, then process it and put it into the regular billing cycle. Knowing your client's customary response period will help you stay calm.

Avoid calling in a reminder before your due date. Clients know when their bills are due, and they're not obligated to pay prior to the due date. Give each client some leeway—at least a week—before calling (see Tip 55).

Deposit your checks immediately. Receiving a check is not the final step. It still has to clear your account. With today's electronic banking, a deposit made to your *business* account is usually available for spending in no more than two business days—and often one. There are three sound reasons never to set a check aside to deposit later: First, you delay access to the funds. Second, you postpone finding out whether a questionable client's check is actually good. Your bank will notify you when a rubber check bounces, but that may take days. To play it safe, call one or two days after depositing a check to see if it has cleared. And third, you avoid losing the check and having to make an embarrassing call to your client asking him to put a stop on the original (the fee for which should be deducted from your balance) and issue a second check.

Cash the check of any suspicious or failing client the same day you receive it. Actually, you should never get into this position in the first place. Some years ago, however, I had a client who suddenly began failing. I had invoices due and was continually calling about receiving payment. Over a short period of time I received several checks drawn on a local bank. I took each check to the bank immediately after receiving it and cashed it instead of depositing it and waiting for it to clear in my account. Someone else might have cleaned out the client's account first. I came out unscathed.

Give proper attention to prompt payment and you'll avoid the headaches of collections. (But since collection problems may be inevitable at some time, see Tip 56.)

TIP 55

Set a broadcast schedule.

Create a system for notifying clients when invoices are past due.

When our children were little, Carolyn and I, like all parents, were often up in the middle of the night. But no problem—at least we knew where the kids were. The day our oldest child got his driver's license was the day we *really* started losing sleep. When he was late, I'd start planning whom to call—friends' houses at 11:30 P.M., the hospitals at 12:30 A.M., the police at 1:00 A.M. As a parent you want to take some control over the situation. As a rational adult, you also want to retain control over yourself.

Overdue invoices create the same set of challenges. Establish a schedule for notifying clients after your reasonable due date has passed—and stick to it. This will help make your collection process more routine and enable you to stay more issue-focused, objective, and calm. Try this:

Ten days overdue—fax. Faxing is faster than the mail, less dramatic than an express courier, and not as harrying as a phone call. A little humor doesn't hurt, either, because it can help prevent angry or awkward feelings on the part of your client. My overdue notice looks like this:

Arf Arf.
Woof Woof.
Bow Wow.

Perhaps the mail carrier, about to deliver a welcome check, was set upon by a dog who, aroused by the scent of chocolate chip cookies baking nearby and lacking the resources to secure one of the tasty morsels, became so upset that said mail carrier was forced from the route designated by the Postal Service and unable to complete his or her appointed rounds. Perhaps not. Either way, please make prompt payment on:

Invoice: __________
Date: __________
Client: __________
Job: __________
Past Due: $__________

Thank you!

Twenty days overdue—phone. If ten days go by and you haven't received word of payment or the check itself, call your client contact for assistance. Include your request for a return call or fax with the status of your payment by the next business day.

Twenty-five days overdue—call your buddy (see Tip 56). If your contact can't help, call the accounting department to cut through whatever red tape or miscommunication may have garbled information between accounting, your contact, and you. Again, ask for a commitment regarding when you will receive your check. "It's on so-and-so's desk" is not a satisfactory answer. Some so-and-so's will hold unsigned checks for weeks.

Thirty-five days overdue—call the CEO. Most CEOs are somewhat removed from day-to-day bill paying and may not know their accounting departments are dragging their feet.

They'll often help move things along rather than have negative word get out about their company. Make your remarks clear and concise. Explain that you've already gone through channels without satisfaction. And offer to fax a copy of your invoice. Is the thirty-five-business-day mark too early to go to the top? No way. That's seven weeks late! You may want to make a little noise even earlier if you're being stonewalled. After all, you're not asking for any special favor; you simply want to be paid on time. When a bill is this late, there's a problem, and it should be *your client's* problem, not yours.

How should you act with everyone you contact? Tip 56 goes into detail. Just remember that you'll maximize your efforts when you rely on a logical plan. Don't fly into a panic and wing it.

Be methodical about collecting overdue invoices, and you'll collect your due in both the short and the long run.

TIP 56

Find a buddy.

Build a good relationship with someone in your client's accounting department to help speed payment when your invoice is overdue.

While I was writing this book, I worked on several projects for a small ad agency in Silicon Valley. When I found that my invoices were past due, I called the creative director who was responsible for hiring me. When I found that he was not well versed in returning calls (he unfortunately is one of many such people), I tried the art director with whom I'd worked. He couldn't help me. So I went to "the source."

I called the accounting department, got connected, and calmly presented my problem. Avoiding a meaningless confrontation, I also suggested that perhaps the agency's cash flow was limited and that a term of thirty days might be difficult, since I always finish my part of an ad or direct mail package before the agency completes the project and bills its client. "That's exactly right," she told me very pleasantly. I responded that while thirty days represented my normal terms, forty-five days would be agreeable to me if it was good with the agency. She said it would be. And it is. My checks come on time. Just as important, should payment be delayed in the future, I have a friendly ally in an important position to assist me. If there's a question of *whom* to pay when funds are limited, I want to be at the head of the list.

You can resolve payment problems without risking your relationship. By all means inform your contact that a bill is overdue. She may be able to exert some influence on the situation to keep you, as one of her key resources, happy. Even if she can't do anything, your informing her of the situation is a courtesy she is due. Client contacts often have no idea about their companies' accounts payable operations.

If your contact can't help you, don't pester her. Ask for someone in the accounting department who will shepherd you through the payment process. Then, use this process to maximize your chances for prompt payment:

Be friendly and polite. You may be miffed that you haven't been paid on time, but you must sound as if you assume that the person you've reached wants to help you. Most bookkeeping people actually do, and they will willingly explain if a computer or other problem has delayed them. They'll also tell you when you can expect payment. At worst, the courteously squeaky wheel will be heard when others are forgotten.

Ask about your new buddy's needs first. Take an interest in the challenges to your client company's ability to pay you and inquire as to what you can do to help make your friend's job easier. You become one of the "good" suppliers and leapfrog ahead of the pack.

Explain your position. Be sure your friend has all the facts. Then ascertain that she has your invoice and that it is complete. Remember, your *right* to be paid isn't an issue. Getting someone to cut you a check is.

Find a mutually acceptable solution. The reality is that you may have to compromise. But if your new friend is willing to act in good faith, give her the benefit of the doubt. Then send a memo to confirm the agreement in writing.

Relay the outcome back to your contact. If your check doesn't arrive as scheduled, you may awaken her to rallying behind you by going to a more senior executive.

If you still don't get paid, notify your contact again, and then go to the top. Call the president (see Tip 55). Let her be embarrassed—or have to explain why her company is so weak she can't pay you.

Be positive, firm, and friendly, and you'll achieve positive results most often.

TIP 57

Avoid vendoritis.

Insist that you be paid independently of your client's financial relationships, and pay your own suppliers on time.

Johnny Carson used to do a great routine on *The Tonight Show.* Dressed as a mystic, he would give viewers the answers to unknown questions secured in "hermetically sealed" envelopes. That piece of business is perfect for this tip: "The answer is . . . 'No.' Now, after opening the envelope, I will reveal the appropriate question—'What do you say to a client who says you'll get paid as soon as he gets paid?'"

I call this kind of client attitude vendoritis. While the word "vendor" simply denotes a supplier of goods or services, it is frequently used as a pejorative—"He's only a vendor." This reflects an unwillingness to value suppliers' services and business integrity. Vendoritis often reveals itself in delayed payment and also extends to such behavior as not responding to proposals, returning phone calls, or dealing honestly and openly with the exchange of information regarding your projects and relationship.

I've been through this. When I first moved to San Francisco, my one acquaintance—a producer of industrial films—asked me to write a radio commercial campaign for an agency of the U.S. government. I did. And month after month he explained to me that the federal government is a notoriously slow payer, and that I'd get paid when . . .

Yes, I got paid—about eight months later. And I vowed I would never work that way again. The reason is simple. A client's relationship with you has nothing to do with that client's relationship with anyone else. The client who hires you bears *sole* responsibility for paying you. The only exception involves clients with whom you have a personal relationship or one who proposes a reasonable agreement that delays payment to a set, and mutually agreeable, date (see Tip 54).

You can't always prevent vendoritis, but you *can* prevent it from keeping you from getting paid. What's more, you can halt its spread to help protect yourself and other freelancers.

Make it a standard, "no exceptions" practice that payment for your services is your client's responsibility, not anyone else's. Discuss appropriate terms and stick to them. Failing to do so encourages clients to treat you poorly in *every* aspect of your business.

Assume responsibility for your own suppliers. Never order any work you can't pay for out of your own funds. Billing on estimate or in advance (see Tip 50) can help. Aside from doing what's right, you'll build firmer relationships with your suppliers. When an emergency crops up, you'll find them far more willing to respond with enthusiasm rather than excuses. What goes around *does* come around.

Be firm about valuing *yourself* and you'll find that clients and suppliers alike will value doing business with you.

TIP 58

Unleash the dogs sparingly.

Weigh the practical consequences before you call in lawyers or go to court. Sometimes you can lose by winning.

In the movie *A Bronx Tale,* Chazz Palmenteri as the neighborhood Mafia chief tells the impressionable young son of bus driver Robert De Niro to forget about another youngster who owes him twenty dollars. He advises the boy to forget the debt as a cheap way of writing the debtor off. The gangster's statement seems surprising, since he later tells the boy that his business success comes from being feared, not loved. Even a mobster has to be practical, picking his fights carefully and staying detached from situations that might inflame the desire for revenge.

When a client owes you money, you may wish to break his legs, but you'll probably fall back on the American credo: "I'll sue." Before you consider doing that, however, you may wish to try everything else in your power. At worst, you'll end up writing off the debtor as well as the debt.

I once had a problem with a major catalog retailer that had moved its headquarters from the East Bay to San Francisco. Struggling financially, the retailer failed to pay me and two associates. By the time the matter became critical, my client contact had left the company. Over a period of time, my associates and I sent faxes to the company's chief financial officer and phoned repeatedly, but we never received a response. I decided to contact the president, a major investor in a number of Bay Area businesses and someone who might have been embarrassed by the situation. But before I did, one of my associates got word that the company would issue us checks. That associate and I notified the client that we would go to their offices to pick them up, and we did so without delay.

In spite of his efforts, the other associate never got paid. He could have gone to court, but he realized it would have cost him more to collect than to drop the matter. But none of us ever dropped the matter completely. Of course, I can't tell you who this client was—even though I study Hebrew with the language cassettes they originally gave me. But I do still spread the word among other freelancers as to this client's deplorable behavior.

A San Francisco advertising agency specializing in promotions for major national clients once took the same attitude toward paying me for a job that I had completed—and that they loved. I could have gone to small claims court, but I stuck to the process detailed in Tips 54 and 55. Finally, a fax to the agency's president was evidently embarrassing enough to merit payment.

But what do you do when everything else fails?

Check your local and state laws carefully before you go to small claims court or any similar judicial entity. These courts hold hearings for claims typically under $1,500 or $2,000 and can render a judgment requiring your client to pay. However, you may not be able to recoup the value of the time you spend preparing for a hearing and attending it. Also, critically, the court may not be empowered to enforce its decision. You already knew your client owed you money. Getting the client to pay you was the problem in the first place. You may not need legal sanction to claim a moral victory. A friend once went to small claims court and couldn't get paid, but he did value learning from the experience.

Determine the total cost before you launch a lawsuit. If the stakes are high enough, you may want to consider legal action. An agency client of mine successfully recovered over $100,000—minus legal fees, of course. But do realize that your lawyer will end up with a fairly hefty portion of your award. And the time and expense necessary to see your case through will cost you as well. Regardless, you may still come out ahead. But if a firm letter from your attorney—and perhaps a willingness to arrange a series of payments over time—will get the job done, you may decide to forgo the thrill of quarrying your prey in a courtroom. If not, go get 'em, and good luck!

As a footnote, I must state that persistence can pay off. In the late 1980s, a designer and I worked on a catalog for an electronic games distributor. The client declared bankruptcy before we could get paid. I soon forgot all about it. The designer—a determined and successful businessman—went through all the paperwork required to stake a claim on the company's assets. In November 1996 he sent me a check for $69, my half of our award, representing a small fraction of our fee. (That, by the way, is integrity! He could have kept the few dollars and never notified me.) We went out to lunch at a Chinese restaurant, one of his favorite places, and blew $5 each. The rest was pure gravy. But I do wonder whether he received more than a dollar an hour for the time it took him to follow through on the matter.

Whether money or principle is your motivating factor, stay as objective as you can when considering legal action, and you'll give yourself your best shot at meeting your objective in the end.

Chapter 8

MASTERING MEETINGS

American business seems to run on meetings. However, I often think that it's a miracle American business doesn't run *down* on meetings. I attended a meeting once at a large corporation. The key contact was late for the meeting because she was in another meeting. Another contact explained that the staff spent most of their days in meetings, so they arrived at work at seven in the morning to get something done before the meetings started, stayed late to do more, then took work home. Had this book been published at that time, I would have given her a copy.

Most people dislike meetings. They're generally too long at best and useless at worst. But meetings are inevitable, whether you're a freelancer or an employee. Of course, there is one difference. As an employee, your company pays for your meeting time. As a freelancer, you can pay dearly when you can't control the length and quality of your meetings—or find other ways to communicate when a meeting is not necessary.

Meeting skills are simply crucial to building your freelance business. Since you can't avoid meetings, you must *control* them. And you *can*. The tips that follow will help you save time and energy while maximizing outcomes. I'd tease you with even more in this introduction, but I have to go to a . . .

TIP 59

Take charge of the face-to-face.

Consider every meeting an exercise in diplomacy and an opportunity to enhance a client relationship.

In 1993 Secretary of State Warren Christopher shuttled throughout the Middle East and Europe to encourage Israel and the Palestine Liberation Organization to sign the Oslo Accords. Israeli Prime Minister Yitzhak Rabin and PLO leader Yasir Arafat then flew to Washington to meet with President Clinton, shake hands before the world on television, and personally sign their historic agreement.

As a freelancer, you often have to engage in shuttle diplomacy as well. And while the results may be somewhat less earth-shattering, their impact on your business may be considerable.

A great many businesspeople share my disdain for meetings. That being said, however, bear in mind that there are many times when meetings are truly important, if not efficient. As Finn Caspersen, chairman and CEO of Beneficial Corporation, explains in Joel Garreau's fascinating book *Edge City: Life on the New Frontier,* "you lose that team spirit, the ability to work together, if you don't get that touchy-feely, the face-to-face." Maintaining a positive attitude and taking a high-energy approach to meetings can make all the difference between keeping a client interested in you and losing one.

It works both ways! Clients often need to see their service suppliers in person to feel confident in them. This also offers you, as a freelancer, the opportunity to give your client a better picture of who you are and what you're like. You become more "present" in the client's mind and thus more memorable. In a competitive world, that counts for a lot.

Further, some clients are simply not sufficiently organized to give you all the information you require by phone, fax, and E-mail. They need to be in the same place to feel that they have sufficient time to present a project and their views about it or adequately review work you've done. Conversely, seeing a client's facial expressions and body language and hearing his vocal inflections can help you understand what he wants, likes, and needs—or fears and dislikes. I've spent a lot of time just watching clients who *weren't* speaking to gauge their position on an issue (see Tip 63).

Of course, not all meetings are formal. And you can take additional time before or after to socialize. Small talk can pay big dividends in developing rapport and trust. What's more, to save travel time you can piggyback meetings that take place any distance from your office.

You should know, however, that a meeting is necessary in some circumstances:

When you're being briefed on a major project. The bigger and more demanding the project, the more complex your information-gathering becomes. A meeting can make it easier not only for your client to brief you but for you to ask lots of questions in person and receive background materials to take back to your office.

When your contact's manager or a senior executive is involved. Maybe the boss will provide you with an overview or details. Or maybe she just wants to sit in. Conference calls are only so effective. And meeting your contact's boss can be very helpful, since she's the one who will ultimately approve your hiring and fee estimate.

When a client team is involved. I've sat at conference room tables facing half a dozen client contacts, five of whom did not need to be present for me to get the job done. But *they* thought they had to be there, because each had an interest in the project. Since each person on a team will pass judgment on your work, you want to understand everyone's individual needs and, above all, find out who the heavyweights are so you can gain their confidence. If politics is a business, business is politics!

When a client is nervous or concerned. An agitated client is a dangerous client. It doesn't matter whether his jitters are justified or not. When a client seems concerned, pay a house call. Your presence can go a long way toward alleviating the symptoms and the problem behind them.

You may never come to love meetings, but if you recognize that they often satisfy the client's needs, you'll find ways to make them satisfy your needs as well.

TIP 60

Practice alchemy with time.

Determine how much meeting time a project will require and include that time in your estimate.

One afternoon an ad agency art director calls me and asks me to work on a project. "But first," he says, "let's meet tomorrow." His office is an hour away—if traffic is light. I know we could handle the briefing by phone and fax, but he strongly believes we should get together. "Can we do it at eight in the morning?" I ask. I'll have to leave home before seven, but that's okay, since the meeting will cut into a busy day if we start any later. "No," he answers. "I never get in before nine." I shrug, unseen by him, and pencil a nine o'clock meeting into my calendar.

The next morning I arrive on time. The art director greets me in the reception area. We never make it to his cubicle or to the conference room because he stops right in the hallway, gives me some rambling briefing papers, and starts talking about the magazine ad we're to do. While we stand. Without coffee! This is *not* my idea of the way a meeting should be conducted. I suggest we sit. He takes the hint and leads me to his cubicle. Then he starts tossing around ideas. I counter with questions, since I still know nothing about the client, the product, its competitive advantages, or the competition's products. He's still way ahead of himself. An hour and a half later I have the information I need. He's happy.

I'm happy, too. Why? Because he's *paying* me to meet with him, and the meter's been running all the while. The longer he talks, the more I earn—even though I'd prefer to cut the meeting short.

Meetings may sometimes seem extraneous, but they are necessary evils, which means that both you and your clients have certain obligations. Bear three things in mind:

Your time is valuable. You can't work on someone else's project when you're in your car or in a meeting room. You must earn a minimum return for the time it takes to get to a meeting and take part in it. (See Tips 43 and 46 regarding minimum fees.)

Meeting time is working time. No meeting requested by a client or needed by you is ever incidental. Meetings are work, not play. If they weren't important, you wouldn't be getting together. It only makes sense that you get paid for your time.

Your client's time is valuable. There's a flip side. I've heard of several charlatans who scheduled numerous meetings and dragged them on so that they could bill for their time. Professionals *earn* their fees. If you request a meeting, be sure it's necessary. Then be sure you follow Tip 62.

Know your worth, and every meeting will represent time well spent by you and money well spent by your client.

TIP 61

Make an impression.

Do as your parents taught you. Stand tall, smile, speak distinctly, and remember that the business side of every meeting starts with the first hello.

Carolyn and I are normal parents. When our children were younger, we reminded them to wash their hands, tie their shoes, look people in the eye, and speak loudly enough to be heard when introduced before welcoming people to our home or going to a social function elsewhere.

When they became teenagers we reminded them to wash their hands, tie their shoes, look people in the eye, and speak loudly enough to be heard when introduced—and maybe wear jeans without huge holes in the knees—before welcoming people to our home or going to a social function elsewhere. They've done pretty well, because relating to people properly is often a learned trait albeit one that doesn't always come easily.

At this point, you may feel a little put out with me. You'd never go to a meeting and act like a child. And yet I've been to countless meetings in which experienced adults—caught up in the tension or the excitement surrounding a project—somehow managed to forget all that their parents had ever taught them.

Perhaps a client can afford to be less than neat, friendly, polite, and considerate. You, as a freelancer, cannot. No matter how brilliant your core skills, you will ultimately be judged on the way you relate to people in challenging settings. Making a good impression, however, is really simple, because what we learned as children still applies:

Arrive on time. If you've ever been kept waiting by a client, the buyer of your services, you know how unpleasant that can be. Put the shoe on the other foot, and you can understand what a disaster lateness can be for you, the seller. Determine how long it will take you to reach your meeting. Then leave earlier. It's better to spend a few minutes listening to the car radio in a parking lot or reading a magazine in a lobby than to leave a client waiting. In addition, plan a little extra time to get from the parking lot or garage to the lobby and then to the meeting room. Arrive in the lobby or reception area five or ten minutes before your meeting is scheduled to start. Other clients may be waiting for you in a conference room—clients with schedules at least as hectic as yours. "On time" means ready to work. Just as important, phone if you're running late. If you have a cell phone, no problem. If not, take an extra few minutes to go to a pay phone and notify your client in advance. Your courtesy will be appreciated and your problem understood.

Dress appropriately. Every industry and every company has its own standard for dress, and that includes casual Fridays. If a suit is standard, wear a suit. If jeans are the norm, slacks or jeans will blend right in. However, you can still dress to play a role and get away with it. I often dress more casually than my clients just to live up to my image as a creative person. Best of all, I can get away without wearing a tie when others can't.

Prepare yourself. Get as much information about your client and the project as you can before the meeting. Then bring along the tools of your trade—anything from a large, thick pad for note-taking (never bring out a pocket-size pad or loose sheets of paper, since these indicate that you don't expect to hear much of importance from your client), extra pens or pencils (if you have to borrow a pen, you'll seem scattered), and even a cassette recorder if you don't want anything to get past you. No matter how you're dressed, no matter how sociable you are, there's a time to look all business.

Share coffee. If you're offered something to eat or drink, accept it, even if you take only one sip. People bond over food and drink, a custom that goes back to ancient days and is common to all peoples.

Stand when you meet a client. In our informal society, people rarely stand anymore when they meet others. Once, men always stood when a woman entered the room (sexist by today's rules) or when they met older people (ageist these days). But standing shows respect for the person who has hired you. If I'm sitting when a client twenty-five years younger enters a meeting room, I'll stand to say hello. It's not self-deprecating to indicate that you appreciate the opportunity to work for your client and acknowledge her authority within the parameters of the project.

Introduce yourself and your associates clearly. Smile. Look your client in the eye. Shake hands firmly. Speak your name slowly. State what you do and why you're attending the meeting. And remember the people you've brought with you. I've seen many experienced businesspeople introduce themselves and forget everyone else on their team. State each associate's name and what each one does.

Give your business card to everyone. Americans and Canadians come from so many different cultures that people in meetings are always hearing unfamiliar names. It's important that clients know your name and how to spell it. Your card will help. Likewise, ask everyone for a card so that you can know all your clients' names and spell them correctly in memos, faxes, and other correspondence. As small a matter as it seems, misspelling a name can alienate someone, not so much because it shows disrespect—which it does, in a small way—but because it indicates carelessness and laziness. Our names are precious to us. We need to treat others' names kindly by taking the time to get them right.

Turn off your cell phone or beeper. Every meeting deserves your undivided attention. You can check your beeper or voice mail as soon as the meeting ends. If you anticipate a personal emergency, give your client's phone number to a family member beforehand, or ask, prior to the meeting's start, if you can make a call at a certain time.

Put your best foot forward, and you'll take a step in the right direction every time.

TIP 62

Hone your game plan.

For every meeting you hold, choose the right participants, define objectives, follow a carefully timed agenda, and leave everyone enthusiastic.

Chances are that you, like me, have attended meetings that have occupied entire mornings or afternoons. On occasion, the volume of information was so great that the meeting truly required several hours. Most often, however, the person conducting the meeting had simply not prepared very well. Matters were left open-ended, requiring lengthy discussions; important information was not researched; perhaps a key player was not invited.

Whether you need to hold a meeting with associates or ask for one with clients to get a project off to a better start, you can maximize the outcome and minimize the time spent by organizing first. You'll gain a reputation for effective meetings if you take these steps:

Make sure a meeting is necessary. We often assume that people need to sit down around a meeting table every time a project is undertaken or reviewed. Frequently, distributing and gathering information by E-mail, fax, and telephone will do. In some cases, though, a meeting can really help get a project off on the right foot—and speed the project along—when everyone gathers at once, hears the same information presented in the same way, and focuses on achieving the same agreed-upon result in the same way.

Determine your objectives. Decide what you want the meeting to accomplish, and be *specific.* Broad goals like "increase sales" or "make a more dynamic impression in the marketplace" will not guide participants in working on the project. Define budgets, timetables, competitive situations, areas of responsibility, available resources, and parameters for workable ideas.

Choose your participants carefully. Invite everyone who has a key role to play in the project. Leave out those on the periphery unless they are supervisors who may need an initial briefing or must be called on to enforce guidelines so that your project stays within bounds. Based on the complexity of your project, decide whether it is better to have everyone involved attend the meeting or to hold two or more meetings with different groups. If you can include everyone, do it to ensure consistent communication and promote teamwork across the board.

Find the right time of day. If you're not a morning person, you'll lead your meeting more effectively if you hold it in the afternoon. If afternoons are usually hectic, get started first thing in the morning with the time based on the distance attendees have to travel. You can often squeeze a meeting into a busy day by holding it over lunch—a *light* lunch that won't put people to sleep.

Serve something. I never hold a meeting without offering refreshments. My usual explanation is "I'm Jewish, so a meeting without food isn't official." The reason for serving food is simple. Sometimes people get thirsty. Sometimes they get hungry. Often they become both. If you're planning a two-hour meeting to start at eleven in the morning, serve lunch at noon and work through it. If you're meeting at four or five in the afternoon, bear in mind that people will be thinking about dinner. Remember, too, that people always draw closer together around food. Setting a warm, welcoming tone will help you break through potential interpersonal barriers at the outset.

Gather all background materials. Since you've defined your project at the outset, gather all the materials participants will need and have copies ready for each person. Giving everyone the same information will provide participants with a broader perspective, including an understanding of each team member's responsibilities. This will also save time, since participants can start working as soon as the meeting ends.

Create and follow an agenda. Decide on the length of the meeting in advance so participants will know when they can move on to other tasks. Then budget your allotted time with an agenda that carefully schedules all of the meeting's components. For example:

9:00–9:10	Introductions and coffee served
9:10–9:25	I present overview—history of challenge and project as conceived
9:25–9:40	Jason presents competitors' solutions
9:40–9:45	Claudia reviews ground rules regarding timing
9:45–10:00	Paul discusses production guidelines
10:00–10:20	General discussion
10:20–10:30	I review individual tasks and deadlines, then conclude

Outline your presentation. At least the first part of your meeting will be devoted to providing background on your project and bringing everyone onto the same page. Make clear, concise notes so that you can cover all the bases in the least amount of time necessary to communicate.

Set individual outcomes. A meeting is effective only when each participant has a clear idea of what he or she is supposed to do afterward. Be sure that you make each individual's responsibilities clear and reassign tasks when necessary.

Organize your meetings enthusiastically, and you'll conclude them with all participants enthusiastically united and ready to make your project a success.

TIP 63

Play fly on the wall.

Listen to others first, observe their body language, zero in on the real decision-makers, take notes to support your position, and then speak up.

A well-known graphic designer with whom I used to work told me an interesting story some years ago. He was redesigning the pumps for a major gasoline company, and his client asked that he make the logo bigger. Without commenting, the designer sketched a larger logo on a drawing of the pump. The client wasn't satisfied. The designer quietly sketched an even larger logo. "Bigger," the client insisted. Of course, a gas pump occupies a finite space, and the placement of various components limits the area that can be devoted to graphics. The designer, after complying several times and listening actively, finally said, "What you really want is for the logo to be more prominent." The client beamed and declared, "That's right!" The designer again sketched the pump. The logo was no larger than it had been in his first design, but he had changed other graphic elements to make the logo seem more powerfully present. The client was happy. So was the designer.

Meetings are a lot like horse races. Most participants want to bolt out of the starting gate to impress everyone else, assert their importance, and gain a sense of control. This is not a selfish impulse—only a normal, and sometimes foolish, one. But anyone who's ever seen horses, automobiles, or people race knows that it's not where you start but where you finish that earns the wreath of roses or the bottle of champagne, not to mention the big money. In general, you can contribute more to a meeting to which you've been invited by listening and observing first.

I liken sitting back and observing to leading troops into battle. The motto of the army's Infantry Officer Candidate School at Fort Benning is "Follow me." But a platoon leader rarely leads a charge unless a situation is desperate. If your troops are behind you, you can't control them. In meeting-room battlegrounds, you give up a lot when you lead with every thought and opinion you have before you've drawn a picture of what confronts you.

I admit that there's an element of manipulation in all this. But there's nothing underhanded about holding your tongue until your comments can be more finely honed. Through their comments, voice tone, and body language, people generally reveal their strengths and weaknesses. As a fly on the wall—an observer—you are well positioned to identify the decision-makers and the potential troublemakers. This information allows you to develop an instant strategy for winning over those with power and then letting *them* control participants who may not agree with you.

Here are some ways to maximize your impact on meetings:

Say as little as possible at the outset. Have your suggestions and solutions ready, but be prepared to amend them if necessary based on the tenor of the meeting. You'll consistently impress people as someone who is thoughtful and always on target.

Profile each participant. By observing how people react to each other, you can quickly determine whose influence is greatest and who is likely to oppose your suggestions. You can also decide how best to influence the decision-makers to get them on your side.

Take notes. Don't rely solely on your memory. Write down any meaningful comment so that you can later refer to it and, if necessary, identify the speaker. This will send a clear message to everyone around the table that you are on top of all the details and highly credible.

Stay flexible. Sometimes the ideas you bring to a meeting prove to be right on target. Other times, changing parameters or personal tastes will indicate that you need to rethink your contributions. By waiting, you can assess whether the comments you were initially prepared to make are appropriate or whether you need to stake out a different position. You may not always come up with solutions at a meeting, but you will always avoid leading yourself up blind alleys.

Be tactful. Observers are shrewd and calculating rather than quiet. When you speak, be deliberate, polite, and seemingly impartial. Give logical reasons for your solutions, acknowledging what others have said that supports your conclusions. And above all, avoid contentiousness. You can win more allies through reason than through antagonism.

Defer to the power brokers. When the decision-makers take your side, be silent. Let them praise you without responding and without taking credit for your solutions. Your value will be perceived. If they override your opinions, accept their authority. As long as you initially present ideas you believe to be in your client's best interest, you've done your job. Clients always retain the right to make the final call.

Playing fly on the wall demands both restraint and an exquisite sense of timing. Hold your tongue and observe at first, and you'll later observe your influence in meetings growing considerably greater.

TIP 64

Assume the controls.

Step in when a meeting starts wandering. Focus on objectives, foster decision-making, and encourage reasonable time constraints.

We've all seen movies in which dissatisfied crew members—on anything from a sailing ship exploring the Pacific to a space cruiser crossing a galaxy—decide that their voyage is not proceeding as anticipated and plan a rebellion. In most military services around the world, the penalty for mutiny is death. When you attend a meeting that is floundering, however, you don't have to commit a felony to help correct the situation and avert a fiasco that could undermine the success of a project.

While I was planning this book, the general manager of an ad agency that had called on my services proposed a meeting at 5:00 P.M. A group of agency staff members and freelancers would review concepts for a retail ad that would soon run in major newspapers and magazines around the nation to promote a new computer printer. The schedule was tight, and the GM, who didn't mind working evenings, wanted to speed the project along. I know few people, myself included, who like to attend meetings at the end of the workday, so I suggested to the agency's creative director that dinner be served as a means of picking up the group's energy level. He agreed and passed on the suggestion. When I arrived at five, I found that the agency had provided not pizza or sandwiches but a complete catered buffet, from salad to dessert. The ten or so people attending the meeting were so pleased by the agency's thoughtfulness that their resentment about having to meet at that time was cast aside.

With everyone in a good mood, we began reviewing the concepts by placing numerous layout versions of the ad on tables and walls. Suddenly the meeting became bogged down. The group had come up with a number of interesting ideas, and the agency account people began debating each concept at length. It appeared that we were in for a long evening.

Realizing that we were not making progress, I suggested what should have been obvious—that we first eliminate the concepts no one liked or to which the client might have logical objections (they needed no debate) and post on the bulletin board the concepts everyone liked (these too required no immediate discussion). Then we could turn our attention to the rest. Reducing the number of concepts for review would make our choices less bewildering, and we would already have arrived at a number of sound solutions, lessening the pressure and confusion. The process of selecting or rejecting the remainder of the concepts and arriving at final choices went quickly. Everyone was satisfied, and the meeting ended at a reasonable time.

As we tidied up, the general manager commented to me, "You'd be a great account coordinator." I could have replied, "I run a business. I have to make sure that meetings go well," but I demurred and simply responded, "Thanks."

You can come to the rescue when a meeting gets out of hand. Your success will depend on *what* you recommend and *how* you do it. To steer a meeting back on course without disrupting it, remember these tips:

Be polite. No matter how far others have wandered, remember that confrontation doesn't solve problems. Modest suggestions ("Perhaps we should consider . . .") work far better than demands or commands.

State the positives first. Begin your suggestion with acknowledgment of what the meeting has accomplished: "It's really helpful that we're all here," or "Mary's suggestion for saving time will really help us." This provides a foundation on which to build and lessens fears that the meeting is doomed to failure.

Restate the meeting's objectives. This will help to restore focus on the purpose of the meeting. Remind everyone why the meeting was called and offer ways in which the group can get back on track: "Roberto hit on something when he talked about where the market is headed. Let's review who our customers are and why they want what we're selling."

Keep an eye on the clock. Both leaders and participants often get wrapped up in details that would be better left to one-on-one discussions or that are not relevant to the task at hand. These people forget the time and leave the rest of the participants squirming in their seats and tuning out dialogue that usually ends up being a one-way conversation. This presents you with the perfect opportunity to say, "Excuse me. I see it's twenty to three and we still haven't dealt with a couple of important issues. Perhaps you could work this out later."

Keep an eye on all the participants. By observing participants' reactions, you'll be able to gauge whether or not the meeting is working. Body language offers a major clue as to when people have lost interest and are going through the motions or will not come to agreement under existing conditions.

Save complaints for private conversation. If something is obviously wrong with the meeting, suggest a short break so that participants can regroup. Sometimes an adjournment to the next day is called for. But speak to the leader about what went wrong, and suggest ways to improve the meeting only when you have a chance to be alone—face-to-face or on the phone.

Turn to positive yet subtle suggestions when a meeting is veering off course, and you can turn a meeting around quickly.

TIP 65

File after-action reports.

Write and distribute memos that confirm decisions made in meetings you conducted or make clear your role following meetings you've attended.

When I was creative director at an ad agency in San Francisco, my responsibility was to maximize the impact of our ads and commercials. But the work of one of our account executives was valued even more highly. He was a memo writer. What he lacked in quality he made up for in quantity. That impressed the agency's president, if not the rest of us. Some time earlier, I had been sent to the grand opening of a savings and loan branch in the San Joaquin Valley—a carnival-like activity designed to lure a big crowd. The agency owners were so impressed by my follow-up memo recommending that we scrap the grand opening event, which drew more children on bicycles than savers, that they asked me to become an account executive. I declined.

Anyone who's ever received an E-mail message and noted the list of people to whom it was broadcast knows that American business can go memo-crazy. And yet a memo can serve to document the basic agreement arrived at by two or more people and can serve as a valuable guideline for future action. While the creative side of me could live without memos, the business side of me knows that memos—concise and utilized judiciously—can protect my best interests by eliminating the potential for future confusion.

When you hold a meeting, follow up with a memo to all attendees so that everyone can follow the same guidelines and schedules. Here's how:

Take good notes. Listen to what others have to say and write down your own comments as well so that you can refer to what you actually said, not what you *think* you said.

Write your memo within twenty-four hours. With the meeting fresh in your mind, you can organize your information correctly and include as many nuances and helpful suggestions as possible.

Keep it brief. It's easier to write a long document than a short one because you can just let the words flow without disciplining them. But it's easier to *read* a short memo. Edit your first draft until you've included all the basics but *only* the basics. Make every word count.

Distribute your memo immediately. The most brilliant of documents is worthless until it's shared. E-mail, fax, or mail your memo as soon as possible to keep everyone informed and prevent anyone from getting a head start in the wrong direction.

Invite responses. This accomplishes two important things. First, it encourages participants and others related to the project to ask questions so that everyone is clear on concepts, goals, responsibilities, timetables, and budgets. Second, lack of response indicates acceptance of your memo. That makes it much more difficult for naysayers to find fault with your conclusions long after the meeting—or even the project—has been completed.

Keep your memos. Whether you retain your original electronically or on paper, file it away for future reference to support your position or simply to use as a benchmark to measure progress and results.

Reversing the situation, you will frequently receive memos from clients or associates whose meetings you have attended. Bearing in mind what I've just suggested, be sure to:

Read all memos immediately. It's not sufficient to *think* you know the general agreements produced by the meeting. You need to know how your client or associate has interpreted them officially. You might find principles or instructions in writing that don't necessarily reflect your memory of what was said.

Ask questions. Call, fax, or E-mail the sender as soon as you discover anything in a meeting memo that puzzles you. If the matter is small, make a note on your copy of the memo so that you'll have a lasting record of the correction or decision. If the matter is important, respond with a memo clarifying your position. This will establish the validity of your interpretation of the matter.

As a freelancer, your business is providing an important service, not writing memos. But above all, your business is doing business well. Take the time to write succinct, accurate meeting memos, and you'll enhance your chances of meeting your business objectives.

Chapter 9

WINNING NEW BUSINESS

After three years in the army, I found myself at age twenty-five as rudderless as I was when I graduated from college. I even went to a nearby McDonald's to seek temporary work, although the manager mercifully understood my situation and turned me down.

Soon after that I signed on with an encyclopedia company to do sales. A printed set of encyclopedias is a worthy product (this was before our age of CD-ROMs and the Internet—although bound volumes are still a valuable resource). I took a brief sales course consisting of several evenings studying the product and the company's up-to-the-minute sales techniques. The course itself was worth my time (there was no fee, either), because I've used some of those principles—including always asking for business—as a freelancer.

Having completed the classes, I understood the whys and hows of selling encyclopedias. But the sales manager could not provide me with the personality needed for cold-calling potential customers. I went out one morning and knocked on a door. A woman responded. She wasn't interested. I went home. My door-to-door sales career died a quick and relatively painless death.

I looked into selling insurance, too, but instead ended up teaching school for a year. And yet . . .

And yet I enjoy making presentations to prospects, and I love selling myself and my freelance business. It's just getting to that point that's tough—something like an actor hating auditions but loving to get a part. Contacting people you don't know can be difficult for even the most outgoing people. It still is for me, although less so than it used to be.

My freelance business has grown basically through word of mouth, but in the beginning I did have to contact people. Sometimes I received leads, as I do now. Often, after postponing the task for days or weeks on end, I called prospects cold and asked for an opportunity to show them my samples.

Getting new business is far and away the most difficult challenge a freelancer faces. This chapter may not make you feel comfortable beating the bushes, but it can help you increase your success rate. And success *can* make you feel more comfortable and in turn lead to more frequent and greater successes. Like a journey of a thousand miles, momentum first requires a single step.

TIP 66

Put on the greasepaint.

Play the aggressive new business developer by assuming an actor's attitude toward mastering a role. Then be sure you don't lose yourself in the part.

Although I'm pretty much of an introvert, I love to perform onstage—just as many actors are fairly retiring in their private lives and many comedians are anything but funny away from an audience. Appearing in plays at summer camp and in college did not make me ready for Broadway or Hollywood, but it did give me a better understanding of how to play a part. And in seeking new business, most freelancers truly do have to act their way to success.

Interestingly, the best new-business people I've known aren't actors at all; finding and bringing in new business is what they do—and love—best. They tend to be quite glib, make a terrific first impression, and really enjoy the thrill of the chase. Once the business is secured, however, they often lose interest and detach themselves from the account. They generally don't like the detailed follow-up required to actually conduct a new client's day-to-day business. So as specialists, working with others, they go from one new business project to the next. Your role as a freelancer is far broader and therefore more difficult. You have to cover all the bases—winning new business and then servicing it.

To step into the experts' new-business shoes, you have to play the role. If you don't take to it naturally, you'll need to prepare as an actor might:

Understand your motivation. I once cast an actress for a TV commercial in which she was to play a policewoman who had pulled a car over for speeding. (The driver would have known that the speed limit had been changed if he'd listened to the client, a news-radio station.) The actress asked me what her motivation was. Thinking that the eight-second vignette I'd written was fairly straightforward, I replied, "To get paid." She got the point. And she was great, as expected. As a freelancer, *your* motivation is the same. It's just that simple. Hunger works!

Draw on your inner strength. Remember your belief in yourself (see Tips 1 to 5). Stanislavsky's method requires you to become the character you're playing. That's easy. You're an independent businessperson. And since you've been courageous enough to go out on your own, you can certainly approach any prospect without experiencing stage fright.

Script your cold telephone calls. Many actors love to improvise. Most are trained to do so. But that technique can kill you on the phone. *Know* how you're going to introduce yourself. If you think you might get a little tongue-tied when you try to reach or connect with a prospect, actually write out what you'll say, then read it, if you must. (My son Seth once did this when he had to call a glass company about making a repair for which he was responsible. He read so naturally that I later used him in a radio commercial for Pacific Bell.) And remember to *state your name* when you begin. I frequently get calls from other freelancers seeking work who start, "I'm a writer . . ." and never identify themselves. They don't make much of an impression.

Avoid the hook. Some actors aren't happy unless they're in every scene and have every line. Bear in mind that the time you spend seeking new business is time you're not working on projects. Like a dog chasing its own tail, you can end up spending all your time pursuing new business and never having time to *do* business. Which leads to the next piece of advice . . .

Keep your existing accounts in the spotlight. Make the business you already have your first priority. Take the time to do each job as if it will be the one by which your business will be judged. Often that's exactly how the drama—and sometimes comedy—of freelancing is played out. The easiest and most profitable new business you ever get will be additional jobs from satisfied clients. Build your existing business sufficiently, and you'll rarely have to worry about playing the new-business expert.

Get yourself ready to perform, and you'll increase your new-business performance dramatically.

TIP 67

Plan your attack.

Develop a new business plan that sets reasonable goals while maximizing your use of time and financial resources.

My wife, Carolyn, and I had a very short honeymoon back in 1969—two nights in Houston. I had a teaching job to report to and Carolyn had senior year college classes. But we had already decided to travel through Europe after her graduation, a trip we undertook only after a reasonable amount of planning. We did not have a rigid itinerary. But we did develop a plan that made sense and made the journey more fun.

Since we were traveling from September through December, we set a route that would take us to Scandinavia early in our trip, when the weather would be best, and let us visit the warmer climates of Italy and southern France as late-autumn cold approached. We also researched and purchased Eurailpasses for three months' unlimited first-class train travel that ultimately took us from London to Vienna, southward to Rome, and westward to Madrid, with a great many stops in between. We set a budget, so we knew what kind of lodging we could afford—hotels in the \$5- to \$8-a-night range, breakfast included. Being young, we had no problem with bathrooms down the hall and a lack of room service, which we couldn't afford anyway. We also carried a guidebook on budget travel and consulted it before every departure to take advantage of recommendations for hotels, restaurants, transit, and sight-seeing. We stayed as long as we wished in each place, set out when we wanted to see a new city, and spent three wonderful months exploring.

Seeking new business takes pretty much the same planning effort. It's always great when new business walks in the door from a referral, but actually casting your nets for new clients can seem impossible unless you plan, plan, and plan. Years of sometimes successful (and sometimes not) new-business effort lead me to recommend that you take a few steps:

Set reasonable objectives. Determine how many new clients you can expect to bring in over a period of three, six, and twelve months. Translate that into billings and income as well. If you're just starting out, you don't want to handicap yourself with new business goals that may be impossible to obtain. It does take time to build a business. If you've been freelancing for a while, look back over your prior efforts and decide what results you should expect without creating undue pressure that might distract you from the success you're already enjoying. Remember, your present clients deserve your primary focus. Remember, too, that tenacity and perseverance will see you through over time.

Define your prospects. Anyone who has ever needed the kind of service you provide is a potential client. That stated, it would seem logical that business should fall into your lap like ripe plums from a mature tree. (I use this analogy because the Santa Rosa plum tree in my backyard used to be so laden with fruit that branches would simply fall to the ground.) But where do you start? That question can be paralyzing and can keep you from getting your new-business program under way at all. So start by establishing a profile of clients *you* are best suited to assist (see Tips 69 and 70). Include such details as company size, areas of specialization, and geographic location. Then identify which traits are possessed by the kinds of clients you feel will best build your business, bearing in mind that the biggest companies do not always constitute a freelancer's most attractive market (see Tip 69). Now determine how large a geographical area you can serve. If you can work exclusively by phone, fax, and E-mail, you can pursue clients anywhere. If you need to meet regularly, your clients will have to be able to afford fees large enough to justify your travel time and expense.

Identify the specific individuals you want to contact. There are a number of ways to do this. They are discussed in Tip 71.

Set your budget. Sometimes getting your foot in the door is as simple as making a phone call (see Tip 73). I've often found it more advantageous, however, to establish my identity by mailing something to a prospect before I call (see Tip 74). But what do you mail? A letter? A brochure? A box of interesting trinkets with a letter, a brochure, and a postcard bearing your return address and a stamp? How many mailings do you send to a prospect? And how many prospects do you contact by mail? It all depends on what you can afford. And what happens when a prospect says she'd like to get together with you? Can you afford lunch or a trip out of town? How elaborate a presentation can you make? What materials can you leave behind? Obviously the answers to all these questions will depend on your individual circumstances. But the concept of budgeting is common to all our new-business needs.

Schedule your program. The hunt for new business is extremely challenging and therefore easy to put off. You've got to make a commitment, and that includes a time frame for planning your strategy, identifying prospects, making initial contacts, and following up with them (see Tip 78). You can also use this time frame to approach prospects whose names you've picked up from the media or from associates.

Analyze your results fairly. You want confirmed projects to come out of your new-business campaign. Sometimes you'll do better than you thought. Sometimes you won't. On the one hand, don't assume that because a new-business strategy worked once it always will. On the other hand, don't assume that a strategy that fell short in the long run has to be dismissed out of hand. Review what you did and why you did it. List the techniques that worked well and those that didn't. And keep your chin up if your initial efforts provide more kind words than hard dollars. A foot in the door may not pay the bills now, but it can lead to profitable business relationships in the future, provided you maintain contact (see Tip 78).

Set your course carefully, and obtaining fruitful new business will become a matter of course through the years.

TIP 68

Position yourself.

Create a unique impression that sets you apart and clearly identifies why a client should hire you.

Some years ago the advertising industry fell in love with a "new" concept known as *positioning*. A number of experts writing in the trade media announced that creativity—how eye-catching, dramatic, or amusing an ad might be—would be far less important than establishing a product or service's relative position in the marketplace against those of its competitors. Consumers would respond most enthusiastically when they understood a product to be "the first," "the best," "the fastest," or "the most economical."

The flurry of words about positioning soon faded away. Yet positioning has never disappeared, because it has *always* been the cornerstone of good marketing and advertising, bearing a variety of names over the years. You need to position yourself correctly in order to answer a prospect's most basic question: "Why should I do business with you instead of someone else?"

Several decades ago, confronted by Hertz's dominance as the nation's largest car rental company, Avis positioned itself as "number two." This took some courage, because most advertisers want to be seen as the biggest and most prominent in their fields. By positioning itself against every competitor *except* Hertz, Avis very successfully nudged aside all other car rental companies without losing credibility. Furthermore, Avis's slogan, "We try harder," also took a clever poke at Hertz, giving consumers a reason to believe they would be better treated by "hungry" Avis than by the satisfied leader, which would rest on its laurels. The campaign worked. Americans like scrappy underdogs.

Freelancers also need to position themselves. It's tempting to say that you can do and be virtually everything and anything (see Tip 8). Perhaps you can, but clients need a better sense of who you are if they are to distinguish you from your competitors. By creating a more specific impression, you can truly stand apart.

A word of advice: whatever position you establish, make sure you can back it up. Exaggerating your claims in order to get a job can cost you in the long run if you can't do the work as promised. In this regard, I go back to the conflicting theories on the demise of Piels beer in New York some years ago. The TV commercials for Piels were cartoons featuring the characters Bert and Harry. The commercials were very clever, appealed to a broad spectrum of people, and were not at all typical of beer advertising that targets blue-collar "Joe Six-Packs." Ultimately, however, Piels went under. Savants blamed the advertising. But a thoughtful writer later brought forth the theory that the advertising *had* worked. Beer drinkers *did* try Piels in large numbers—only to find out it wasn't very good. Piels sales plummeted as a result.

How can you position yourself successfully? Consider these variables, then focus on those that *best* represent you and your work:

Quality. How does yours compare to that of other freelancers? You don't have to be the most brilliant in your field to be good and to produce results for your client. Be self-confident—and be honest!

Speed. Can you get the job done faster than others, particularly in rush situations? Remember, speed and quality don't always go hand in hand. What does your market demand?

Price. Are you less expensive than the competition? What kind of client is looking for the lowest price, and will a low-ball position keep you from getting better-paying jobs? Is price the major consideration in your market? You can certainly position yourself as *competitively* priced—a useful generalization—without giving part of your fee away. If you're very good with a lot of experience, you can position yourself as relatively expensive but worth the price. Some clients offer their respect in direct proportion to the size of the fees they pay. They *assume* that only someone who charges a high fee can do the work they require.

Dependability. Clients can always find cheap work, but it may not meet their needs. They can pay a lot for brilliant work as well. But will they get it on time and to their specifications? Being able to get the job done right and on time—even when deadlines are tight or conditions are difficult—can help you stake out a reassuring position.

Experience. You may well impress prospects if you have had experience as an employee with a major firm in their industry or if you count big companies among your clients. At the same time, midsize prospects may be impressed that you've worked successfully for or with companies of their size and understand the challenges they face with smaller budgets than the giants provide. Or you may be a small-business expert who knows firsthand the resource and budget constraints small companies face and can move projects ahead under those conditions. If you have more than one area of expertise, you can focus on each specific prospect's needs, positioning your experience differently to different-size companies.

Enthusiasm. Perhaps you have an outgoing personality that encourages people to work with you. By all means, translate that into "service with a smile," "a great team player," "making business a pleasure," or a like position, which should be reflected in both your work style and your communications materials. Chemistry—an attraction for purely subjective reasons—plays a major role in client decisions, even though most clients will never admit it. (See Tip 77.)

Of course, you can combine any number of these elements in any number of ways. You can create a slogan or just an overall impression that positions you against your competitors. Once you've done so, let that position be the platform that communicates a consistent message. In my mailers to clients and prospects, I want to get across a simple premise: *on time, on target, on budget.* I want to be known for my professionalism. I also frequently refer to my number of years as a freelancer and list recent clients to enhance my position as an *experienced* professional rather than a young, hungry newcomer who'll accept any fee to get a foot in the door. I know what kinds of clients I want, and I know what *they* want.

Give your prospects a clear picture of who you are, and you'll give them clear reasons to meet with, remember, and hire you.

TIP 69

Put "big" in perspective.

Include smaller prospects in your new-business plans. Many are quite sophisticated, pay well, and can help you build a solid, diversified client base.

American culture has always venerated size. Cities were once proud of their large populations. Reaching the one million mark—or the 100,000 mark for smaller cities—seemed to convey a sense of legitimacy (not to mention heightened business opportunities) to many local citizens. When I was young, Texas epitomized bigness, a quality of which Texans were proud. (Having traveled all across the state, I can vouch for its size.) Alaska's statehood, and then the oil bust, eroded much of *that* legend and eliminated most of it from our national humor.

On the other hand, rising gasoline prices in the seventies and eighties turned the public to small cars. Urban sprawl and environmental perils helped foster the opinion that small is beautiful. When it comes to building a freelance business, valuing smallness can be very important.

I work directly with two Fortune 100 companies and through advertising agencies for a number of Fortune 500 and Fortune 1000 firms. Now that corporate restructuring shrunk the marketing department at one of my Fortune 100 clients—along with the number of jobs they handle—who replaced those billings? Smaller companies.

My advertising agency clients also tend to be relatively small. For a number of reasons the really big agencies just don't constitute my marketplace (see Tip 9). Smaller agencies are my bread and butter, and they've rewarded me handsomely. As you target new business prospects, go after the big guns by all means—but not exclusively. Bear these facts in mind:

Big companies face increasing pressure to cut costs. This works in freelancers' favor, since these companies frequently seek outside service suppliers to minimize staff size. Many projects get scaled back or eliminated, however, leaving a pool of hungry freelancers to compete for a shrinking pie.

Smaller businesses often expand their efforts while big ones are pulling back. These small companies can compete only by being leaner and meaner than the big guys. At the same time, they have to be aggressive and show that they can deliver quality to survive. They represent outstanding business opportunities.

Small clients can be very sophisticated. Downsizing has spawned a great many micro and small businesses headed by former big-company executives and employees. The technology industry, for one, is known for its start-ups piloted by breakaway CEOs or by techies with new and brilliant ideas. These people bring to their marketplace excellent credentials, considerable experience, and a determination to succeed. Catch them early and grow along with them.

We all love to drop names. Major clients can be a feather in your cap and can help you get additional business. But remember that prospecting only at the top can limit your bottom line.

Including small prospects in your search for new business can deliver big results.

TIP 70

Smash the monolith.

Approach large corporations as conglomerations of smaller entities. Then target the people who supervise projects or their managers.

In the early 1990s, I walked into the office of the CEO of one of the world's largest corporations, a multinational with sales in the billions and offices in every major city on every continent. I was there, of course, to do business. The corporation happened to be one of my clients. But honesty—as well as this tip—compels me to make clear that I wasn't working for this huge corporation on that day. Instead, I was working for a small advertising and public relations firm in Silicon Valley that was handling the area's anti-drought campaign. Drought presents a cyclical, and serious, problem in the semiarid San Francisco Bay Area, and the agency had called on me to record this CEO—one of several who had volunteered their services for a radio campaign—asking businesses and residents to conserve water.

Truthfully, I would never have met the CEO, who was quite gracious and helpful, any other way. His corporation is a valued client of mine. But the people I deal with occupy positions many levels below those of the company's senior executives. My contacts at this client are project managers scattered all around the country from the Bay Area to Chicago, Dallas, and Washington, D.C. I've never even met most of them.

If you think of a major corporation as a monolith with your entry requiring access to the executive suite, you may find your efforts quickly frustrated. The key to getting into major corporations is what financial people term "drilling down"—getting below the top layers. You need to target project managers and department supervisors.

Project managers are generally the *influencers*—folks who directly handle projects, often coordinating the efforts of a variety of related project managers, and who will serve as your primary contacts. However, they usually cannot make the decision to contract for your services without approval from a superior.

Department supervisors are the *buyers,* low- or mid-level managers generally one level in authority above the project managers. They may be present when you make a presentation, but often they will have little or no contact with you once your project has begun. However, these managers authorize your hiring and approve your fee. They also frequently evaluate the work you and your contact do.

How do you find these people? The task can be formidable! My contacts at my multinational client started with a small advertising agency that left me free to deal with its local contact in matters pertaining to copywriting. When the agency failed to provide adequate service relating to its own responsibilities, the contact asked me to take over additional functions while she handled the rest herself. Happy with my work, she passed my name on and entered it into the company's list of approved suppliers.

What can you do to get your foot in the door of a major corporation?

Speak with anyone you know who is an employee of a large company. Explain what you do and what kinds of projects you wish to become involved in.

Ask for referrals. You may end up chatting with people who aren't remotely connected with your area of expertise. But they may know or be able to point you toward contacts who can help you. Keep asking those new contacts for additional references until you reach a project manager or supervisor who can hire you.

Target assistants, not department heads. This often requires intensive drilling down and the patience to match, but it works. If you're a programmer, for example, you can call the office of the executive vice president for information systems or, better yet, the management information systems director who occupies a rung below the EVP/IS in the corporate hierarchy. These senior executives generally won't be available to you, but their assistants (there are no secretaries anymore) may well be accessible. Identify yourself and your goals, and ask whom you should contact. You may have to track your way through a number of subsequent calls to get to the people you're looking for, but you'll make more headway than if you try to sell yourself at the top.

Big corporations can be as frustrating as they are tempting. Cut them down to size, and you'll increase your opportunities to grow.

TIP 71

Go the private eye route.

Gather all the information you can about prospects from friends, associates, and the media. Keep your files current, and refer to them frequently.

When I opened my freelance business, I had been in San Francisco for five years. That was certainly long enough for me to get to know a number of people in ad agencies, media firms, and radio and television stations. So I did what came naturally. I told them that I was now freelancing, and I asked them to let me know when they ran into any accounts I could help with.

Business didn't exactly rush through my door. But developing personal contacts is like cultivating a garden. You fertilize, seed, water, weed—and wait. Sooner or later, green shoots pop up from the ground and grow. Within two years, several creative directors I had contacted at major ad agencies—people who never asked me to do a freelance job for them—were calling me on occasion to ask if I would work for clients too small for them to handle.

It's really easy to overlook the obvious, but new-business prospects often stare you right in the eye. Build your list through:

People you know. A close associate of mine handled several major accounts at a direct response ad agency. Over time, he decided to form an agency of his own with a staff of one—himself. He mentioned his departure to his clients. Two of them asked if he would handle their business. He hit the ground running! You never know who can provide a valuable referral, so it pays to tell everyone you can that you're starting a freelance business or currently running one. Chat with fellow employees, vendors, clients, friends, and relatives. Word does get around.

Professional groups. Being a somewhat shy and retiring type, I've never been much for joining clubs and becoming involved in their activities. But becoming better known in your field is always a plus, and that can happen if you choose the right organizations. A former client of mine once referred me to the Stanford Alumni Association, which had been holding day-long workshops for communications professionals. Because I enjoy teaching, I presented copywriting workshops for the association for several years. One student, a marketing manager, ended up becoming a client of mine at three different companies!

The Yellow Pages. Let your fingers do the walking as you check the Yellow Pages for the names of companies that might need your services. Enter their addresses and phone numbers into your database, and then start calling them. In my early years I created a list of small agencies to approach regarding radio commercial production. I managed to set a couple of appointments. One resulted in my being asked to do a campaign for a shoppers' newspaper in Southern California. It proved both profitable and fun.

Trade publications. In these periodicals you'll find up-to-date news about new companies, about existing firms that are expanding their activities, and about new personnel and promotions relating to the positions you need to contact.

Newspapers and magazines. General and business publications also provide news about companies as well as people, their titles, and their activities.

The Internet. So who doesn't have a Web page today? Maybe *you* do. You may not find the names of project managers and supervisors on the Net, but you can learn a lot more about a prospect and do valuable homework to prepare for a scheduled presentation (see Tip 75).

Observation. It's not uncommon to discover a company you might want to approach while you're out driving or walking. Businesses that are just opening can prove particularly fruitful, since you may get your foot in the door before your competition. Stop if you can. Note the name and address. Go in if possible and ask to speak with someone, or at least leave your card. You have nothing to lose, and even a business that doesn't need your services could end up producing a referral.

When you have identified a prospect, add it to your database. Keep names, addresses, and phone numbers updated. Then contact the prospects on your list periodically. A rejection today could become a hot opportunity next week or next month.

Keep on top of potential prospects, and you'll keep your new business efforts moving toward greater success.

TIP 72

Mine your clients.

Ask contacts in large organizations for referrals within their organization and in other companies.

Some of the best new-business leads I've ever received were from existing clients who referred me to others within their organizations. I had this experience with a major technology company. My client contact was very enthusiastic about my work and referred me to other managers within the company. In time, those managers gave me the names of still more people to call. A very satisfied client in a second major corporation also referred me to another project manager.

The trick, of course, is to know when to ask for a referral and when not to. These guidelines will help you:

Ask if providing referrals is all right. Some clients may feel uncomfortable giving you names, either because releasing such information violates company policy or because they don't want to be responsible for fellow employees being solicited. If the latter is true and your relationship is good, you can ask your contact to call a potential prospect and ask if the prospect's name can be passed on to you.

Keep your contact free from compromising situations. Client contacts compete with their peers for the limited number of promotions available in their companies. A contact who really values you as a resource may want to keep you to himself, since you serve as a competitive advantage. If your client contact seems hesitant in this regard, withdraw your request.

Express your thanks when you get a referral. Saying thank you seems to have become a lost art these days. A call—or better yet a handwritten note—truly makes an impression. Avoid sending your contact a gift of considerable value, however. In many corporations, this constitutes breach of policy. Even if it doesn't, it could compromise your contact's integrity in the eyes of his manager, supervisor, or peers.

Be gracious if your contact refuses to give you a referral. If your contact declines to pass on your name for corporate or personal reasons, thank him anyway and conceal any disappointment you may feel. Your contact may or may not offer an explanation. If he doesn't, refrain from asking for one. You'll be putting him on the spot—not a good way to maintain a healthy relationship.

Respect the fact that referrals are made solely at your contact's discretion.

Use your contact's name when you call a prospect. Leverage the personal nature of the referral to maximize your chance of getting through (see Tip 73). Be positive as well. "Joan Smith at Brown Company suggested I call you" offers a far more powerful opening than "Joan Smith at Brown Company mentioned your name."

Express your thanks again after you speak with your prospect. Call or write a note regardless of the outcome. Your contact will probably want to know the results, and you'll take advantage of another opportunity to express your appreciation and build your relationship.

Wait until your relationship is solidified with a new contact before asking for a referral. If the client company is large enough, you can go through a whole chain of referrals. But bear in mind that the best clients are the ones you already have. If you ask for a referral too soon, your aggressiveness may leave the impression that you're not really focused on your new contact's needs.

Seek new business from your existing clients in order to turn up additional clients with less effort and at less cost.

TIP 73

Turn cold into hot.

Prepare before you phone a prospect. Then identify yourself clearly, and make a strongly positioned statement right at the beginning.

Stockbrokers call me at my office from time to time. They don't know me, and I don't know them. Since I handle my own investments, I politely thank them for calling and tell them I'm not interested. I find it fascinating, however, that almost all of these brokers, who may be just starting in the business, since they're cold-calling people like me, seem not to have a clue about communicating effectively on the phone. In fact, their telephone manner virtually disqualifies them from consideration as soon as they speak.

Whenever I let these conversations go on longer than a few seconds, I am amazed not only that most of these brokers do a poor job of interesting me in the securities they want to sell, but that they often—quite inadvertently and unknowingly—end up insulting me, their prospect, as well. For example, in response to my "No, thanks, I'm not interested" I frequently hear, "Well, if you don't want to make more money than you're making now . . ." I may have a number of reasons for not wanting to do business with a broker—perhaps my funds are already tied up or I'm exploring other opportunities—but deliberately choosing to make less money, all other conditions being equal, is not one of them.

If you're at all like me, you don't relish making cold calls. In fact, I almost always send a letter or mailer to a prospect first unless I've been given a name as a referral. And I'll often send a mailer to referrals before calling to establish my identity prior to picking up the phone. But with or without a mailed contact, your first call to a prospect who doesn't know you is still a cold call. How can you help get a prospect to warm up to you?

Clearly—and slowly—state your name and then position what you do. In the excitement of reaching a prospect, it's easy to start rambling right from the opening "Hello." Yet it's vital that your prospect hear your name, not a mumbled sound. Your name, when understood, establishes you as a person with an individual identity and helps to legitimize your call. It also indicates trustworthiness. A muffled name suggests that you have something to hide or are not who you purport to be. Take your time, repeat your name if you sense your prospect has not heard it clearly, then let your prospect know what you do and why you are worth listening to: "Hello, I'm David Perlstein, a freelance copywriter with over fifteen years' experience in direct mail for some of the most impressive names in technology." (See Tip 68.)

Tell your prospect why you're calling. Do this immediately, and include in your statement what you'd like your prospect's reaction to be: "Hello, I'm David Perlstein, a freelance copywriter with over fifteen years' experience in direct mail for some of the most impressive names in technology. I'd like to speak with you about setting up a meeting at your convenience so that I can introduce myself and show you some of my work. That way you can count me as another professional, dependable resource available to you."

Overcome objections. Give your prospect a chance to answer. If she's interested right away, you can set an appointment. If she mentions reasons why she's not interested in meeting you, *empathize* with her, and then turn the objection into an advantage:

PROSPECT: I don't need any more freelancers.

YOU: You must have made a lot of contacts in your work. But with vacations, illnesses, and rush projects, you never know when you'll need to call on a truly professional and dependable freelancer. I'd just like to set up a brief meeting to help you add to your roster.

Time constraints can also keep prospects from wanting to interview freelancers. Again, empathizing can help you.

PROSPECT: Sorry, but I'm very busy. I just don't have the time.

YOU: I certainly understand how busy you must be and how valuable your time is. We're all pushed to the limit these days, aren't we? But I'd just like to set up a brief meeting at any time that's convenient for you.

Ask for a commitment. It's natural to wait for a prospect to say, "Okay, let's get together." But you'll do better if you offer your prospect two or more choices, any one of which would satisfy *you:* "I'd just like to set up a brief meeting, and we can do it any time that's convenient for you. Would you prefer first thing in the morning or later in the day?" Once your prospect agrees to one of your choices, you can set the date and time: "First thing is fine. Eight-thirty or nine? . . . Tuesday or Wednesday?"

Remember your goal. What you really want from a cold call is a meeting, not a job. Few prospects hire freelancers sight unseen. You therefore want to remind your client that you don't expect a firm commitment. You just want to introduce yourself. Later, as you conclude your meeting, you can—and should—ask for business.

Be flexible. Offering a prospect the opportunity to decide the date, time, and place of your meeting is a smart way to let your prospect stay in control—under your guidance. That means, however, that you must be prepared to meet whenever and wherever your prospect wishes. You're the seller. She's the buyer. Meet her demands.

Stay in touch if you can't set up an appointment. No matter how effective your telephone manner and how strong a freelancer you are, you won't always be able to set up an appointment with a prospect. In other instances you may decide, upon speaking with a prospect, that she's not worth meeting with. But if she is, advise her that you'll forward some printed materials—a detailed letter, résumé, client list, brochure, samples—whatever will help to convince her that she should see you or hire you. In your letter or note, refer to the date of your call and explain that the enclosed materials are the ones you promised to send her. This will create the structure of a mutual communication and take the first small step in establishing a de facto relationship.

Call again in thirty or sixty days. One rejection doesn't mean that the book is closed. Prospects often have lots of suppliers or truly are too busy to meet. But illnesses, vacations, new business, company growth, policy changes, or simply a better mood can alter a prospect's attitude toward seeing you. Follow up politely, again overcome her hesitation, be agreeable in the face of rejection, and mail a letter or note thanking her for taking the time to speak with you on the phone. You could well get a call from her six months or even six years later. It's happened to me!

Mix careful preparation with personal warmth, and your cold calls can heat up your new-business program dramatically.

TIP 74

Make the "write" move.

Mail letters, postcards, or packages to acquaint prospects with you. Your options are infinite as long as each piece looks professionally done.

Small investments can definitely yield big dividends. Years ago I began sending humorous self-mailers—one-fold postcards—to clients and prospects. Being a copywriter, I created each one with a clever teaser headline on the outside, then witty copy inside that explained how I could help meet their needs. My goal was simple: to acquaint prospects with my copywriting skills by demonstrating the quality of my copy on the mailer they received. I hoped they would be responsive to my follow-up phone calls, keep my mailer in their files, or at least store my name in their memories for future reference. Existing clients would enjoy a chuckle while being reminded that I was available to them.

Over the years these mailers—produced inexpensively—have worked well. Periodically, I receive a phone call from someone who received a mailer years earlier and now has a job for me to do. With some frequency, in response to a mailing, a mailer—or just my name—has been passed on (sometimes two or three times) to someone who has called and become a client. And often, existing clients call with new jobs right after a mailing goes out. I believe this is always more than coincidence.

My most successful mailer began reaping rewards over ten years ago. The tease line on the outside asked, "Why is great copy like great pizza?" The copy inside explained my point of view: "There's plenty of both around, but the good stuff is really hard to find" and "A pizza maker will cook up a whole pie or serve you just a slice. David will conceptualize a whole campaign or write a single TV or radio spot, a/v script, direct mail piece, or ad." It also stated that I would bring along a large pizza when the prospect called to set up an appointment, "Because there's nothing better than a pizza joint—or writer—that delivers." I got one immediate response—and it paid off handsomely!

The day after I dropped a hundred or so of those mailers in the box, a prospect called. I'd worked with him previously when he was at a major direct response ad agency but had lost contact when he set up a shop of his own. He told me he needed immediate help. I brought the pizza, and we got started on the job. In the years since, we've worked together steadily, and my total billings with him have surpassed $300,000. That's a pretty good return for a mailing that cost less than $125 including postage.

However you put it to use, direct mail is a great medium for reaching prospects. It lets you introduce yourself without interrupting your prospect, who is free to read the piece at her leisure. The mailer is tangible, so it can remain in a prospect's view, either left lying on a desk or pinned to a bulletin board. It can be photocopied and passed on to your prospect's associates. And it enables you to communicate your individual personality while providing necessary details about your qualifications and experience.

Direct mail doesn't have to be expensive, either—just well planned and neatly executed. And you can take any number of approaches:

Business letter. Think a letter is a bit dry? Few people even write letters today, let alone write them compellingly. A letter can exhibit a great deal of professionalism, particularly to conservative prospects in conservative industries. And you have many options. For example, consider sending your letter in a bright-colored 9- by 12-inch envelope to grab a prospect's immediate attention. You can enclose your résumé, client list, samples or photocopies of work you've done (this can include photos and drawings as well as the first page or two of a report or white paper), and a copy of an article about you that appeared in the media. If an article about your industry supports your particular talents, you can include that.

Self-mailer. I prefer mailers for blind prospecting, and I send them out—on 8½- by 11-inch card stock coated on one side and folded in half—three or four times a year. I set the type on my Macintosh, do the illustrations, and have them photocopied on a huge machine that makes them appear to have been printed—even to professionals. My cost for a hundred or so to be copied, scored, and folded is usually under $75. I simply address them, add a brief personal note, and attach a first-class stamp to each. You can create almost any size and type of mailer based on your budget and creative resources. Be sure you check with your local post office if you're putting together something in an odd size.

Dimensional package. Sometimes an envelope can get lost on a prospect's desk, but a box containing a letter and other appropriate materials can really pique your prospect's curiosity. A designer I know in Arizona couldn't figure out how to contact prospective employers and get noticed in a very competitive market until I suggested placing a note ("I'm thirsting for great design challenges") inside a water bottle inside a mailing tube with an SOS signal in Morse code on the label. It wasn't expensive, but it was effective.

Express delivery package. I don't know anyone who doesn't open a FedEx, UPS, or DHL Worldwide letter immediately. There's more expense involved, but if you've targeted a few prime prospects, this is a great way to get their attention and show that you're a serious businessperson.

However you approach direct mail, you'll enhance your opportunities by remembering the basics:

Be neat and professional. You don't have to be an advertising or design pro to do this. But you *must* do it. In the business world the medium is at least half the message. Word processing makes professional-looking letters, résumés, and the like a cinch. Just make sure you use appropriate type fonts that are neat and legible. (Save the fun stuff for personal use.) Draft and redraft your letter until it's as perfect as you can make it. And check the spelling!

Get help. Call on a copywriter or designer if you can afford one, or trade services with a professional to ensure that your mailing will make the impression you've intended.

Be provocative! Get your prospect interested as soon as she spots your mailer on her desk. Your envelope and address panel or mailing label should carry a headline that teases your prospect sufficiently to make her want to take the next step—opening and reading your mailer. But a word of caution: your tease line or a headline (Johnson box) atop your letter should *always* relate to your core message and always be in good taste. No one wants to attract the wrong kind of attention.

Position yourself at once. Separate yourself from the competition by stating the competitive advantages you offer. Your entire mail piece—or campaign—should be built around your position (see Tip 68).

Be credible. Include a mention of clients you've worked for and projects you've completed. This will give your prospect an idea of your experience and capabilities that goes beyond mere promises. If you're just starting your freelance business, refer to your experience as an employee. If you've had no experience at all, design your mail piece so that it reflects your abilities regarding communication and problem-solving.

Address your prospect's needs. Naturally, your mail pieces will focus on your abilities. But those abilities are valuable to your prospects only as they relate to furthering their interests. Link your skills to meeting your prospects' needs.

State your expectations. If you'll be calling prospects to follow up, let them know that. Either way, ask your prospects to call you or to E-mail you or visit your Web site.

To maximize your success, follow up with a call about five days after you mail your pieces. You'll have broken the ice and become something of a known quantity. If you're sending out a large volume of pieces, stagger the mailing dates so you have time to make your calls without deferring your other tasks.

Without question, direct mail can be a complex medium. This tip has not attempted to give you the short course in direct mail expertise. But these basic principles can guide your direct mail efforts in the right direction.

Use letters and other direct mail media correctly, and you can write new business faster than you may have ever expected.

TIP 75

Pitch strikes.

Prepare and rehearse your presentation, keep it brief and lively, and always focus on your prospect's needs.

If cold-calling is like auditioning—and few actors like to audition—then making a presentation is like appearing on Broadway. An audience awaits, and you are the star of the show.

But all great performances require a lot of preparation. Even a brief and informal presentation has to be well thought out, since your first impression may be your *only* impression. Whether you'll be meeting with a prospect for ten minutes or for an hour, you will make your presentation more dynamic and effective when you remember these guidelines:

Know your prospect. If your prospect is a businessperson, find out what his company does. Get a brochure if you can (asking for one by phone is fine), look over a sample of the prospect's work, research trade or general media, or go to your prospect's Web site. If your business involves providing a personal service, briefly ask your prospect about his needs and concerns in advance.

Rehearse. If yours is a formal presentation, script and rehearse it to make sure you get in all the information you want to communicate at a reasonable pace and within the time available to you. Then *speak,* don't read, when you actually present; reading is wooden no matter how good you are. If your meeting is casual, outline what you want to say and how much time you'll need so that you won't get bogged down or distracted. Gather and sort through in advance any materials you'll want to show.

Dress appropriately. Determine what your prospect is likely to wear, and dress correspondingly. I wear a tie and jacket when I see prospects in the financial realm but a jacket only, possibly with jeans on dress-down Fridays, when I go to technology companies or ad agencies, where informal dress is the rule. If you're not sure, dress up rather than down. You can always remove a tie, jacket, or scarf. Then put on your best smile, shake hands firmly, and look your prospect right in the eye.

Ask if others should attend your presentation. Sometimes a prospect will hear you out before deciding to have you come back and meet with his coworkers or supervisors. By asking if your prospect would like someone else in the meeting, you may reach a key decision-maker at once and speed up the process of turning a prospect into a client. If your prospect suggests bringing someone else in *after* she's taken your measure, give a repeat performance enthusiastically.

Find out if your prospect is under a time constraint. You may need forty-five minutes to present yourself—a time period agreed upon in advance—only to find that your prospect has only half an hour available. Be prepared ahead of time with a more concise version of your presentation so you can communicate all the important details no matter how little time you have.

Accept something to drink or eat. My father once gave me a bit of advice from a salesman's perspective: always have coffee with a client. He told me that sharing something to drink or eat is a key way people bond with each other, a practice common to all cultures. Accepting a cup of coffee or tea, a can of soda, or a glass of water can bring you and a prospect a bit closer.

Wake up your meeting at the start. While presentations are no-nonsense affairs, an ice-breaker can grab your prospects' attention when routine business may have them sidetracked. My business card containing my "Flamboyant Logo Goes Here" graphic always gets a laugh and a positive comment. That sets an upbeat mood and provides me with a confidence-builder. An associate, who was making the last of ten presentations to a major insurance company, asked me to come up with ideas for a way to attract the committee's attention at four in the afternoon. We developed a first-aid kit and filled it with items anyone might need after hearing all those presentations. A box bearing a large red cross held eyedrops, wake-up pills, an energy bar, and more. (My suggestion that we include hemorrhoid medicine was turned down.) The committee got a good laugh out of it, perked up, and listened attentively for the next hour.

Pretest your presentation materials. Back in my ad agency days, I once took part in a presentation to a pizza chain. I had produced an animated storyboard of a TV commercial—illustrations and a sound track—to give our prospect a good feel for our creative thinking. An account executive from our Los Angeles office rented a VCR and a monitor—but never tested the equipment. You guessed it! The VCR didn't work properly, and we blew ourselves out of the water. Nothing we said could overcome that lack of professionalism, and we could only apologize, go through the motions, and fly dejectedly home. Make sure your presentation materials—whether on a laptop or mounted boards—are in working order.

Be concise. As a talented freelancer, you have a lot to say. But prospects have relatively little time to listen. Hone your presentation down to the essentials and include the rest of the details in an attractive leave-behind (see Tip 76).

Stay in control. When you're presenting information about yourself, keep the focus on *you.* If you're using audiovisuals, reveal only two or three short phrases on each screen, slide, or board. These should consist of key words only, since you'll be explaining each in more detail. You want your prospect to concentrate on your spoken words, with printed key phrases or words reinforcing what you say. A prospect who has to read your screen or boards can't always follow what you're saying. Keep track of the time as well. It's easy to get involved in friendly chitchat and side issues. You don't want to run out of time before you've made all your points.

Shift the focus to your prospect. Once you've explained what you do, how you do it, whom you've done it for, and why you should do it for your prospect, ask your prospect to tell you about her needs and expectations, how her company works, what will help make her work go more smoothly or make her life more pleasant. Give her printed materials with more complete details about you and your work *after* you've concluded your remarks. You don't want a prospect to be reading a client roster or sample of your work while you're speaking.

Ask for the business. No matter how well your presentation has gone, you haven't brought it to a successful conclusion until you've said, "Let me do your next job for you."

Write a thank-you note. Does this sound hopelessly old-fashioned? Believe me, it's not! Unfortunately, the art of writing thank-you notes seems all but a lost one. Fortunately, this will work in your favor. Send a note on a note card (in an envelope) or on your letterhead, thanking your prospect for taking the time to see you. Briefly remind her why you're the right person to call. And again, ask for her business! This note offers you a great opportunity to maintain contact and demonstrate your professionalism and thoughtfulness.

Keep your presentation brief, lively, informative, and focused on your prospect's needs, and you'll present what it takes to sell your prospect.

TIP 76

Leave something of yourself.

Give your prospect a printed document to serve as a permanent reference detailing your qualifications. Include an appropriate novelty if you can.

Out of sight is often out of mind. Given the hectic pace in today's workplace, the impact of a great presentation can dissipate quickly once you've left your prospect. To extend and maximize that impact, give your prospect a printed document at the end of your meeting. This will provide him with a handy resource for reference and to pass on to others.

Your leave-behind will work effectively if:

It fits comfortably in a file drawer. Some people think that this is condemning your piece to oblivion. I suggest otherwise. A leave-behind that's very small will get lost. An oversize piece that doesn't fit in a file folder will ultimately be thrown away, since prospects are not likely to carve out space on their already cluttered desks just for your piece. They do use files, however, since the promised era of the paperless office has not yet begun. For an extra advantage, you can design your leave-behind to function *as* a file folder with a brightly colored tab that will catch your prospect's eye.

It makes a visual impact. Even dry information will work hard for you if you present it in a graphically interesting environment. Get professional design assistance if you need it, and consider it a worthwhile investment, since your printed materials, like you, have to help you stand out from the crowd.

It utilizes professional-looking, easy-to-read type fonts. Cute type is neither creative nor bold, nor will it make an impact. With today's word processing capabilities, any document you produce can make a strong impression while being well organized and highly legible.

It clearly positions you. If you've been reading this book sequentially, you've encountered this principle quite often (see Tip 68). Simply put, you must always make a clear distinction between yourself and your competition. Your leave-behind should quickly establish your unique position in the marketplace and support it with information about your experience, clients, achievements, and, if appropriate, awards.

It includes samples of your work. Once you've presented your work, you want to keep it fresh in your prospect's mind. Reprints, photocopies, photographs, and drawings all help a prospect remember who you are and what you do.

It asks for the business. Just like your presentation, your leave-behind is complete only if it clearly states that you want to work with your prospect and if it asks your prospect to award a project to you.

It prominently displays your phone number, fax, E-mail, and Web site. The easier you make it for your prospect to contact you, the more you'll influence your prospect to do so. Be aggressive about making your intentions clear by making your communications channels simple to spot and utilize.

Want to add a little extra touch? Give your prospect a novelty item that ties in with who you are and what you do. My wife, Carolyn, is a storyteller who also acts in TV and radio commercials and in business videos and films. Since her stage (maiden) name is Power, she frequently offers producers and casting agents a Power House candy bar just to heighten awareness of her name. Whatever your freelance business, you can always come up with a novelty item that works. But be sure that its monetary value is minimal to avoid any appearance of seeking undue influence. A freelancer named Champagne, for example, would do better to give out a tiny bottle of bubble bath ("Bubbly you can really get into") rather than a bottle of champagne.

Offer your prospects a leave-behind that extends your presentation, and they'll have more reason to extend business to you.

TIP 77

Ace Chemistry 101.

Understand that prospects ultimately judge freelancers subjectively and that you likewise must feel comfortable with a prospect.

I've participated in many presentations as part of an advertising agency team (even as a freelancer, I've represented a number of agencies). At the end of every presentation, as we leave the meeting room, one of our group inevitably asks, "How do you think we did?" My response is always, "We did (or didn't do) what we were supposed to do, but beyond that, there's no way to know. Either they liked us or they didn't."

Clients in some industries go through a complicated process to find and evaluate service providers. Freelancers may have to respond to lengthy and complicated requests for proposals and follow-up questionnaires before making a series of presentations at which a prospective client's staff members grade them on dozens of variables. Then, months after the process began, the client chooses a winner—usually the person the client "likes."

While clients often weigh a number of factors when deciding to whom they will award new business, chemistry ultimately affects every decision. Whether you take part in a formal screening process or simply a casual meeting, you can control almost everything but your prospect's instinctive response to you. We've all experienced feeling instantly comfortable with some people and truly uneasy with others. That's chemistry.

If you don't get the job, don't get down on yourself. And don't get angry. You truly may have been the best person available, but the chemistry between you and your prospect—through no fault of either of you—may simply not have been right.

On those occasions when the chemistry is off—your prospect never cracks a smile and seems to regard you with all the joy of a patient whose dentist is about to extract several teeth—

keep your cool to avoid creating an awkward situation that could have a negative impact on you in the future. Do the smart thing:

Complete your presentation with enthusiasm. At the very least, you'll avoid making a negative impression, which the prospect could pass on to others. What's more, some clients simply don't have very well developed personalities—at least not in certain business situations. You might correctly sense a lack of chemistry and still end up with the job!

Send a thank-you note anyway. A lack of chemistry may not ultimately stand in the way of you landing a project. Most importantly, you want to be known as a highly professional freelancer, and your reputation is always on the line.

Keep your antennae sharp. Never let the enthusiasm of a presentation cloud your ability to size up a prospect while he's sizing you up. Every prospect should meet *your* standards if you're to do business together. You know you're in for trouble when a prospect yells at employees in front of you or within earshot, when he mentions or suggests questionable business practices, or if he avoids discussing or committing to your honest estimate and billing procedures. That can turn chemistry sour in a hurry.

Be prepared to leave a bad situation. If you sense trouble ahead, politely but firmly state that you don't think the relationship will work, thank the prospect for inviting you, pack up your materials, and go. No freelancer has to suffer an abusive prospect or be placed in a compromising or no-win situation. Don't waste your limited time and energy trying to prove that no prospect can possibly resist you. Move on to others.

Hold on to your options. Suppose that you make a presentation to a prospect with whom you feel uncomfortable. He later calls and asks you to work on a project for him. You don't want to do it. The solution to your predicament can be summed up in one word: *Don't.* Be polite but firm. Turn the offer down, graciously stating that you don't feel you will have a comfortable relationship—and be done with it. You don't owe him a detailed explanation, and you shouldn't get caught up in a long discussion in which he tries to persuade you to take on the assignment against your better judgment. Moreover, you should never accept a job out of embarrassment. Chemistry really does work both ways, and you have an obligation to yourself to conduct your business with the high level of integrity you've set for yourself.

Understand the highly personal nature of business, and the nature of your new business activities will remain positive and profitable.

TIP 78

Keep in touch.

Follow up initial calls and presentations with additional calls and mailings to take advantage of future opportunities and to secure referrals.

I once got a tip on a prospect—a major health care company headquartered in the Bay Area. I sent out one of my mailers. Then I called. After leaving several voice-mail messages, I got through. The prospect referred me to someone else in her department. I sent a mailer. I called. After several weeks I finally reached that second person and attempted to set up a meeting. She was glad to hear from me but didn't want to get together. I sent samples. Then I called back. She mentioned a few possible projects. Nothing happened. I called back. She returned my samples as requested. I sent her my New Year's mailer. And while I haven't yet gotten a project from her, I vow that I will keep trying.

The freelancers who are turned down most often are generally those who are most successful. After all, those freelancers who lack the talent and determination to succeed on their own tend to opt for another way to make a living. Experienced freelancers know that the first time is not always a charm. Few of us succeed with great frequency right off the bat. That's why baseball players get three strikes before they're called out. And why a hitter who makes two outs in every three trips to the plate still ends up making millions.

Following up with your prospects after a presentation is just part of the game. (You'll find additional approaches to keeping up with established clients in Tips 84 to 86.) Remember, you're in business for the long haul. There's no reason to abandon a viable prospect if you don't make a connection right away. A prospect who can't use you now may require your skills in the future. That prospect may move to another position or even another company and then call on your services. Also, your prospect may pass your name on to others. I've had a number of prospects for whom I've never worked develop new business for me.

Following your presentation:

Immediately write a thank-you note. This advice is worth repeating for any appropriate occasion.

Follow up with a call. If your prospect has indicated when a decision will be made about using you, wait until that date has passed, and then call to inquire. If she has no timetable, wait a week, then call. Rather than putting your prospect on the spot, you can ask if she received your note or a promised brochure and whether she would like more information about you, including references. At the conclusion of the call, again thank your prospect for taking the time to see you, and ask for the business.

Keep your prospect on your mailing list. There are a number of good excuses to stay in touch with prospects (see Tip 84). You can call them periodically to see if their situations have changed, and you can send them updated client lists, news of your recent accomplishments and awards, and samples to add to their files. If you prepare periodic general mailings, send them by all means, not only for the impression they make but for their pass-along value.

Over time you won't convert every rejection into a paying project. But the longer you keep your lines of communication open, the greater your opportunity to get a prospect to say yes.

TIP 79

Insist on pay for play.

Consider the pitfalls of speculative work. If you're willing to work for free, do it only on terms you can live with.

As you enter most bakeries you're likely to come across a plate of tempting bite-size samples. Those of us who have qualms about cleaning the sample plate (no matter how much we'd like to) often find that a taste induces us to buy the cookie or pastry we find so delicious. This marketing strategy makes a lot of sense, since goods are baked in batches and removing a few for sampling costs virtually nothing.

Freelancers don't have it quite so easy when it comes to giving away their work.

Some years ago I contacted a chain of tire stores about doing music for their radio commercials. Their advertising director was open to what I had to say—as long as I agreed to create a demonstration of the music. I wrote music and lyrics, then invested a few hundred dollars in producing a demo track. I was quite happy with it and presented it to my prospective client. He listened, shook his head, and told me he wasn't interested. I ate my investment, although I was able to put the track on my demo reel.

At about the same time I did a demo jingle for a clothing retailer. Again I thought I'd come up with a winner. The client, however, went in another direction. I added another cut to my demo reel and realized I'd been kidding myself.

Doing spec work on your own can be disappointing. An agency client, pitching a technology prospect, once asked me to create two direct mail concepts that we could present at a meeting. Because we would have only a short time to complete the project once it was assigned, and because we had adequate information, he believed we could demonstrate our capabilities and show the client how we could complete the project on time. Our work was well received, but another agency got the job. As it turned out, the prospect was just going through the motions. Company policy dictated that each project go out to bid, but she intended all along to hire the agency she knew. When my agency client was faced with a request to do spec from an existing client, he declined.

While spec work is still very much a major part of new-business campaigns in the advertising industry, more and more people have come out against it—even when they feel they can't afford not to take part in spec presentations. I wholeheartedly frown on spec work by freelancers in any field for a number of reasons:

"Spec" is a synonym for "gamble." You spend your own money to produce an ad, a home-selling strategy, a demo program, or a market analysis that your prospect supposedly needs. But price and value go hand in hand. Clients simply don't value work that's done for free the way they do paid work, so your efforts may not be evaluated or appreciated seriously.

Prospects make no commitment to you. Those who insist on spec work are often not serious about projects at all since the work you will do won't have any impact on their budgets. You simply make it easy for them to be tire kickers—shoppers with no real interest in buying. Unlike you, they have nothing to lose.

Solutions to complex problems require information that spec projects generally don't offer. Supposedly, your spec project will meet a challenge your prospect faces. But no one from a freelancer to a giant corporation can develop an adequate solution to a problem without a prospect's active assistance. You need information and contacts first—information and contacts that prospects often won't provide, since they're not making any investment in the project. There's a good reason why we don't ask a doctor for a diagnosis first, then decide whether or not to become a patient.

Budgets may be unequal and may cloud the issues. Providing a competitive spec pitch becomes complicated when you have to guess how much money it will cost you to outshine your rivals. Spending wars, whether small- or large-scale, often ensue. Money gets wasted. And too often the prospect is swayed by production values—the appearance of a presentation rather than the quality of its ideas.

Some clients steal. This is unfortunate but true. You can do great work only to have a prospect appropriate your ideas without putting you on the job. In fact, clients often write into their presentation rules that any ideas generated by service providers belong to the client regardless of the outcome—a provision that shows no respect for the people on the other side of the table.

Competitive pitches must generate losers. It's simple logic. Only one competitor will win the business you're after. The others automatically lose the pitch and the money they've invested. Of course, there's often one exception: the prospect may decide not to hire anyone after all—but instead to "borrow" the best of the competitors' ideas.

As you've probably guessed by now, I don't do spec. I strongly believe that my track record and examples of my work should be sufficient to demonstrate that I can solve problems. I will occasionally assist ad agency clients in doing spec work—but only after trying to talk them out of it. Since they assume all expenses, I owe them my support.

I will *think* about doing a spec job myself under four conditions you should consider carefully:

The prospect pays a fee. I expect remuneration that reasonably covers my time, effort, and expenses even if it doesn't provide a profit.

All competitors work with the same budget. As long as a budget is fixed and no one can spend more than the prospect allows, the playing field becomes level. However, this is a difficult guideline to control, since many competitors are tempted to spend their own money anyway. A prospect must be willing to disqualify a competitor who overspends—a condition few prospects enforce.

The ground rules are clear and uniform. "Just show me something" won't cut it. Ever. A prospect must clearly define the challenge and establish the parameters within which spec work should be done. Again, this levels the playing field and allows the best ideas to come forward.

The prospect pays for any ideas of mine he uses. A spec presentation offers a prospect the opportunity to evaluate a service provider under fire. It is not a bargain basement source of ideas. If a prospect likes the concepts or solutions I've developed and wants to use them, the prospect pays.

The decision to do spec work involves highly personal and individual judgment. Think first—and again—before you agree to work speculatively, and you'll work out the right conclusion.

TIP 80

Tune up your conflict sensor.

Analyze whether pursuing a prospect will jeopardize your relationship with an existing client, and approach each potential problem openly and honestly.

Some years ago I had a steady relationship with an ad agency whose principal client was a company that created relational database management software. Through a referral, I was contacted by another company in the same field. I went to their offices and met with the department head responsible for their direct mail efforts. Our meeting was friendly, and he was impressed with my work. I realized afterward, however, that even though I had no legal obligation to forgo working with him, I owed my loyalty to my existing agency client and their client. I turned down the offer to work with the second high-tech company—a decision that probably cost me quite a bit of money. But I wasn't sorry that I did so—in those specific circumstances.

Many businesspeople might think me foolish because they believe that loyalty has no place in their business lives. I heartily disagree. And yet loyalty works both ways. Determining when a conflict may harm an existing relationship—or when passing up a prospect may harm your business—is no easy matter. Bear these guidelines in mind:

A steady relationship today is worth more than a casual relationship tomorrow. While retainers are wonderful (see Tip 48), most freelancer-client relationships are based on a handshake. Even if you have your client sign an estimate for every job you do (see Tip 49), that client is under no obligation to hire you again. Technically, you're free to work for your client's competitors. The client is then free to take offense at your doing so and not call on you again. Unless you will be signing a retainer—or are willing to gamble away the client you have in the hope of developing a new relationship rather than a one-shot job—you may want to forgo a conflict.

You can always ask your client. Some clients are very proprietary. Others understand that you run a business and that they have no right to demand that you provide your services on an exclusive basis unless they pay for it. (No client would demand that a printer or office supply vendor not sell to a competitor, but the services provided by these suppliers are often viewed as less personal.) If you feel that your client is open enough, bring the subject up for discussion.

You *can,* of course, work for two or more competitors with whom you have a relationship without compromising your integrity. But you must . . .

Notify your clients if you anticipate a problem. It's worth repeating that most clients understand the limits of the demands they can make on you. It's better to be open than to risk a blowup.

Keep what you learn from each client confidential. This can be a tricky business, but it's of paramount importance when you're handling competitive clients. An old World War II poster promoting intelligence security warned, "Loose lips sink ships." Clients may ask you what a competitor is doing. No matter how general and innocent the question, your best response is always "I really can't say. And I never speak about you to them, either."

***Reveal your involvement in conflicting* projects.** Often the projects you work on for one client have no bearing on jobs you do for another. But occasionally you can be asked to work on projects that go head-to-head, either for a specific market share or in a competitive bidding situation. Depending on your role, you could be thrust into a very difficult situation. Before you do anything else, speak with your clients. Let them know exactly what your involvement is. If they're not concerned—since their own input and involvement will greatly determine what you do—you have no problem. If one or more clients express reluctance, start negotiating, and be prepared to retreat from a project. You might even be forced to yield a relationship. But the outcome will be better in the long run if you're honest up front. In fact, any good client will value your integrity and maintain the relationship.

Bear in mind that there is no conflict when no relationship exists. Perhaps a client calls on you only occasionally. Then a competitor who likes your work asks you to handle a project. No problem. Unless and until a client signs a retainer agreement or builds an ongoing relationship that you can't afford to jeopardize, you can work for as many entities within an industry as you wish. Remember, clients may call on a great many other freelancers as well. Every job is an individual one in these circumstances.

Make honesty and integrity the bases of your decisions about conflicts, and you'll reduce your conflicts while you increase your business.

Chapter 10

MAXIMIZING CLIENT RELATIONSHIPS

Some people love the thrill of the chase (see Tip 66). They're more tickled by selling a new client than by the income that new client generates. Getting someone to choose you can be intoxicating to your ego as well as a sound way to enlarge your client base and profit potential. And yet the time you spend pursuing new clients is time you aren't working and making money.

New clients will always represent growth in your business. But the most important element of any freelancer's success is the clients that he or she already has. There are three good reasons to devote considerable effort to your existing clients. First, they are a prime source of projects, and repeat business is the most cost-effective business to acquire. Second, satisfied clients often provide referrals. They knock on doors for you—doors that might be difficult or impossible to open in any other way. Third, clients who are unhappy with what you do cease being clients. You please them or you *lose* them.

Over the years, I've continually seen clients come and go (see Tip 90 for a discussion of client life cycles). But after all these years, my client roster still includes a creative consultant and former ad agency owner with whom I've been working since the early eighties, a direct response ad agency (mid-eighties), and a major technology company (late eighties). A number of other relationships are at or past the five-year mark. And along the way, I've enjoyed five- to ten-year relationships with other clients as well. Had my freelance business been greatly dependent on finding a new client each week, I'd be an employee today.

Keeping clients demands that you match people and business skills to your core skills. The following tips will provide you with proven guidelines for helping to turn every new client into an established one.

TIP 81

Practice QA faithfully.

Make quality assurance part of every job you do to continually earn your clients' trust.

The late astronomer Carl Sagan became a popular author and television figure by informing the world (as we on earth define it) that we are not alone. Sagan would start with the number of stars in creation—"billions and billions"—then emphasize that if only a minute number of stars were orbited by planets, billions of planets might exist. If only a small percentage of planets proved potentially habitable, millions of planets might contain life—and a percentage of them might harbor intelligent life. Faced with the logic of Dr. Sagan's reasoning, many viewers found it difficult to believe that intelligent beings weren't alive somewhere beyond our observable reach.

Equally difficult as it may be to comprehend, we, as freelancers, are not alone either. But unlike civilizations on distant planets, we compete for survival every day.

First and foremost, your clients will judge you by the *quality* of the work you do for them. "Quality assurance" was a hot term in industry some years back. It emerged as if from nowhere, took the business world by storm, then faded as new programs replaced it. But implementing a quality assurance program is simply another way of saying, "Do it right." And that's something we all learned as children. It's not new, but it is enduring. Take these steps to maximize your QA program:

Maintain your integrity. Make sure that every job you do satisfies your *client's* needs, not your own. Advertising-industry people are notorious for creating ads they can show to other ad people (helpful for job-hopping) rather than ads that will help their clients sell most effectively. And when they're not doing work to please each other, many ad people are courting awards committees instead of consumers. No wonder clients show award-winning ad agencies the door with alarming frequency. (Perhaps that's why I never enter awards competitions and have tossed away the awards I've won.) Every client's bottom line is the bottom line. Work that enhances it is *your* bottom line.

Be loyal. Don't pursue your clients' competitors if that will compromise your relationship (see Tip 80). Of course, no client has the right to ask you to work solely for them without paying you sufficiently. But loyalty cuts both ways. There's a reason why people still repeat folk wisdom like "A bird in the hand . . ."

Stay focused. You wouldn't abandon a diamond mine after extracting only the first 100 carats. Do each job for an existing client as if it were your first. Make an impression every time. And make time to do the job right so that your new-business activities don't erode your performance on any job in progress.

Be sensitive to "make or break" jobs. Every so often, a particular task becomes critical to your client. Maybe the company or individual is under heavy pressure. Or maybe your contact's position is under scrutiny. Whatever the reason, you may need to devote extra effort and attention to these special projects. Be open to your client's sensitivities and respond with all the enthusiasm you can muster, even if it means charging less when a budget is unfairly restrictive, and even if you have to spend more hours and energy than are provided for by your fee.

Respect your client's authority. Your client trusts you to provide the right ideas and solutions. You, of course, believe in yourself and your skills. But sometimes your client's reaction to the work you present is less than enthusiastic. Occasionally your client thinks you've missed the mark completely. Take such criticism in stride. I don't suggest that you surrender your professional judgment. Rather, understand your ultimate responsibility. You must, of course, explain the solution you've offered and defend it. You owe that to your client. But if you can't convince your client that you're right, respect his authority to be wrong. You owe *that* to your client as well. If you disagree often enough, either you or your client will eventually break off the relationship. But if the relationship continues, it must be based on your client's having the last word. That's the privilege that comes with paying.

Keep up with the details. Quality assurance emphasizes attention to more than just the big idea. Quality necessitates doing *everything* right, no matter how seemingly small or insignificant. Check your spelling. Check your code. Keep your printouts, layouts, and drawings clean. Be sure that the pages of your report are in order. Everything you do enhances the validity of the solution you propose and communicates a clear message that you are a professional (see Tip 31).

Make quality a prime concern on every job you do, and you'll improve the quality of your relationships and your profits.

TIP 82

Polish your smile and buff your shoeshine.

Provide the high level of service every client deserves by putting clients' needs first and staying flexible enough to meet them.

When I was a kid, my father spent a lot of time in our dinette long after dinner was over. He wasn't continuing to eat—he frequently finished his meals before my mother even started hers. Instead, with the table cleared off, he got out his loose-leaf binders, put his sales records in order, and prepared to follow up on any questions his customers had the next morning. Dad, who sold springs to the bedding and furniture industry, understood that writing orders was the easy part. He tracked his customers' orders right through shipment and delivery and kept them continually informed of new products, features, and price changes. All of his customers felt that Morris Perlstein made their lives a little easier. And Dad made big money.

In Arthur Miller's *Death of a Salesman,* Willie Loman refers to salesmen surviving on "a smile and a shoeshine." In actuality, every freelancer is a salesman, and it takes more than a smile and a shoeshine to succeed. Every client needs a little hand holding—some need quite a bit. This presents a major challenge. In the movie *Splash,* Tom Hanks remains free to look after operations at the family's wholesale fish company while brother John Candy wines and dines their customers. You, on the other hand, have to play both roles.

Client service takes energy and often resourcefulness, but it cements relationships. Here's how you can keep your clients satisfied:

Put your clients' interests first. Attitude is all. As freelancers, we believe we have more control over our time than we did as employees. That's true but only to a point. It's certainly tempting to tell a client that you simply haven't the time to work on a project, since you've planned a day or two of backpacking or because you spend several evenings each week enjoying western line dancing. But unpleasant as it seems, you can't maintain—let alone build—your business by dismissing your clients in favor of your personal interests. By no means should you surrender your private life, but you must understand that your clients need you most when they're challenged by circumstances or superiors. Respond, and your value soars. Head for the movies, and your value plummets.

Deliver on time. Great work makes no impression if it's provided after your client needs it. Meet your deadlines. Period. End of story—almost. (To continue, see Tip 29.)

Make yourself available. Clients want contact—at their convenience—with the people who provide them with services. When your client wants to chat on the phone, be ready to listen. When your client wants to meet, fit the date and time into your client's schedule. If you have to reschedule all or part of your day to accommodate a client's needs, do it. You'll be inconvenienced from time to time, of course, but your client will appreciate your dependability.

Stay reachable. Not infrequently, clients discover problems—or burst forth with brilliant ideas—at the oddest times. And not infrequently they may want to speak with you after dinner rather than following breakfast and a soul-stirring espresso. No one in business today survives without voice mail or an answering machine, so make sure yours is working. Then check for messages as soon as you get to the office in the morning, whenever you're out of the office, and right after you get home. Trade home numbers with your client when an emergency situation crops up. Even if your client doesn't call you in the evening or on a weekend, the comfort of that safety blanket will knit your relationship closer.

Treat your clients' business as if it were your own, and your clients will keep your business humming.

TIP 83

Set out listening posts.

Keep abreast of what's happening with each client's company, career, office politics, personal life, and in any other area that could affect your relationship.

Some of the greatest battles fought in World War II raged in small office cubicles. Cryptographers throughout North America, Europe, and Asia sought to break the communications codes of their enemies—and usually their allies as well—in order to gain information about troop movements, battle plans, and other command decisions large and small. It is no secret that U.S. intelligence forces broke Japan's Purple Code before Pearl Harbor and that the British unraveled Germany's Enigma to hasten the end of World War II.

When I was at officer candidate school, we were taught to gather intelligence on a simpler level. For sheer self-protection, we were to set out one- or two-man observation posts when we were dug in during the day and to establish listening posts at night. (Today's infrared equipment provides night vision as well.) A combat unit can't afford to let the enemy approach its perimeter undetected.

I'm no fan of the "business is war" school of thought. I've lost friends and acquaintances to combat, but I've never seen a client or associate killed in a meeting room. Yet you as a freelancer need to protect the perimeters that surround your relationships with your clients. If knowledge is power, intelligence-gathering allows you to anticipate future events and take control over potentially difficult situations.

It's simple. You need only to keep your eyes and ears open. You don't have to be intrusive—just aware. Your reward can be a better understanding of your client's needs, attitude toward you, interest in your competitors, and even job security affecting your relationship in the long term. To avoid being taken unpleasantly by surprise:

Listen. We all love to share our wisdom. But you can find out more about the business politics and personality of your client—whether a corporation or an individual—by letting your contact do the talking first. You'll also increase your number of sources by cultivating good relations with everyone you meet, from receptionists to assistants to family members of private clients. Small talk can yield big results.

Ask. At times you may sense that something is wrong and suspect that a project or your relationship could be threatened. Talk to others in your contact's department. Ask them if your contact has been having difficulties at work or at home. This often clears up mistaken perceptions, prevents unwise reactions, and enables you to be more helpful to your contact.

Communicate. If a problem threatens to erupt or has already developed with your client, call and discuss it. If the matter is really serious, take your client to lunch. Let her know that you care about the relationship, and ask her to tell you what you need to do to stabilize it. Also bear in mind that clients sometimes hide difficulties with superiors and company policies, leaving you to wonder why the situation seems so terribly awkward. You may be relieved to find out that your client really does approve of your work and that the source of the problem lies elsewhere.

Preempt. Intelligence is meant to be *used.* It generally takes some time for a problem to reach critical mass in a client relationship. Wait until it's too late—and it *is* too late! Identify an obstacle in its early developmental stages, and you can develop a strategy for action. Does someone on the client team think you present one idea only instead of offering choices? Offer choices. Is your client looking at competitors because she believes your fees are too high? Rethink the quality of your work and your estimates to see if you can offer better value. Respond to your client *before* your client confronts you.

Like marriages, business relationships require constant care and thoughtfulness to get through the ups and downs. Work on knowing your client, and you'll work with your client longer.

TIP 84

Launch your PR.

Maintain contact with your clients through phone calls, lunches, and mailings to encourage the awarding of new projects and to hold off competitors.

Several times a year I send humorous mailers to clients, present and past. Invariably a client will call soon after to thank me for brightening his day and to offer me a new project. This client, who already knows me, just needed a small reminder to move me to the front of his mind. Sometimes months or even years go by before such a client calls again. But one mailer after another helps me maintain my presence in his thoughts.

It takes a healthy ego to succeed as a freelancer. Yet none of us can afford to believe that our clients think more about our concerns than about their own. Out of sight *is* out of mind. No matter how successful your relationship, every client's thoughts most frequently turn to other matters—his boss, a possible promotion, his children's grades at school. But you can't afford to let periods between projects widen to erode your income and provide communication gaps through which competitors may slip—or even brazenly march—to push you aside.

Welcome to the world of public relations!

Projects may be intermittent, but the ties that bind you are continual. So keeping up contact with your clients must be a continual process, too. The means are simple and effective (for a discussion of keeping in touch with *prospects,* see Tip 78). To begin, periodically pick up your telephone and say:

"How are you?" Caring is human, and reaching the humanity in our clients—while exposing our own—can make a positive impression and set the stage for better communications.

"Thank you." Even the most business-hardened client appreciates being appreciated. It's all too easy to take a client for granted. In reality our clients owe us nothing but timely payment for a job done correctly. You can do everything possible to earn a client's repeat business, but you can never expect it as your due.

"Let's have lunch." People are social creatures. In fact, that's what led me to sublet an office in downtown San Francisco after nine years of working at home. What's more, sharing food is one of the ultimate bonding acts. Taking time to get together in a non-business setting can let you express your appreciation and offer you and your client a better opportunity to get to know each other's values and thought processes.

There are times when sharing more objective information can be of great use as well. You can put mail, E-mail, and faxes to good use by sending your client:

News about your business. Discuss an important recent project you've concluded, a major client you're working for, or an award you've just received.

Samples of your latest work. Include what challenge you faced, why you developed a specific solution, and how the project might relate to your client's needs.

Industry or related news. Send a tear sheet or a photocopy of a newspaper or magazine article or notes on a TV or radio profile—even a World Wide Web page reference—to provide your client with new ideas and fresh perspectives.

Personal news. Convey some news about your client's hobby or other interests, or your own, to strengthen the personal aspect of your relationship.

An awareness mailer. An interesting, though not necessarily expensive, mailer can demonstrate your skills and knowledge (see Tips 74 and 78). A brief note will add a personal dimension.

Cultivating the clients you already have takes time. And in some ways it seems less glamorous and dynamic than pursuing and landing new clients. But every repeat project you receive from an existing client *is new business.* Keep your name in front of your clients, and you'll keep your momentum going.

TIP 85

Downplay the Santa syndrome.

Give gifts to clients sparingly. Keep them inexpensive. Take client company policies into account. And never expect a project or favor in return.

For six months or so in the early seventies, I wore two hats at an ad agency in San Antonio. Our broadcast media buyer—the woman who negotiated television and radio schedules—had left. My bosses asked me to handle that job while I continued to write and produce all our advertising. They provided me with a small raise and let me buy a few cheap framed prints to hang on the walls of my office to make a better impression on media salespeople. Meanwhile, they saved a broadcast buyer's salary.

Naturally, I was too busy creating ads to do anything other than smile when sales reps came to call and handle paperwork. Our clients paid for all this foolishness, since my creative work was constantly interrupted and I can't remember ever negotiating a single buy. I simply agreed to prices right off the rate cards and typed up the paperwork. Yet even that enforced largesse wasn't enough for some reps.

At that time, the giving of Christmas presents was routine. Even though I don't celebrate Christmas, I found myself deluged with liquor—a waste of stations' money since I didn't drink then, and I don't now—as well as other items meant to curry favor for San Antonio's radio and TV stations. One radio station rep brought me a black plastic flight bag. His gift was at least usable if less than stylish. But several weeks after the holidays, he returned to pay a sales call and announced, "You got yours. Now it's time for me to get mine." I stopped buying the station.

Business gift giving has decreased markedly since then and for precisely the reasons evidenced by this example. Yet I have sent gifts to a number of my freelance clients as thank-yous or for special occasions. There is no reason why you can't give gifts that keep your name fresh in people's minds and still be within the bounds of solid ethics and good taste. Simply follow the basics:

Be sure you're not violating a client company's policy. Not only has gift giving diminished greatly over the years, but many corporations now prohibit their employees from accepting gifts at all. In the early nineties a San Francisco television station fired a husband and wife for accepting accommodations from *friends* who had some relationship to a story being shot overseas. The entire episode was played out in the newspapers, and the couple remained fired even though no attempt to influence them was apparent. A gift that potentially threatens your client is no gift at all.

Keep gifts inexpensive. Your gift should be a token relating to your public relations efforts, something inexpensive that avoids even the appearance of compromising your client. Along with an associate, I've sent fresh bagels or tins of M&M's to steady clients as a way of saying thank you. These gifts are appreciated but are of slight value, particularly when shared within a department, and they never suggest an obligation. Inexpensive food items, handy novelties, and business-related books are a nice gesture of appreciation. One client of mine, who spent her teen years in

New York, collects small, cheap-looking Statue of Liberty souvenirs. Don't ask me why. But whenever I'm in New York, I look for a schlock item under $5 for her. I truly don't think she can be bought for five bucks.

Give gifts of substance only to mark a personal milestone. Sooner or later a client you've dealt with for some time will get married, have a child, or celebrate a special occasion. You can give a gift of *modest* value when it relates to a personal event (an associate and I split a gift certificate to an outstanding restaurant following a client's wedding). Give gifts to a client's child—to celebrate a birth (I've sent baby outfits to new mothers), first communion, bat mitzvah, confirmation, or birthday—only if you've been invited to a ceremony or party or if you have a personal relationship with your client. Gifts to clients you know only in passing can be easily misconstrued.

Give gifts sparingly. A steady stream of gifts may easily be seen as an attempt to buy business, even if the gifts are modest. At some point your friendly intentions may be misinterpreted.

Avoid anything personal, intimate, or suggestive. This advice seems so logical, but it's easy to forget that yours is, first and foremost, a business relationship. No matter how humorous a gift may seem, good taste always makes good sense.

Make sure there are no strings attached. It's worth repeating that any suggestion of a client's being influenced by your gift can imperil your relationship and even lead to your client being disciplined—and to you losing the business. Think inexpensive, think thoughtful, think commitment-free, and above all, *think.*

The business gift isn't dead. But years of abuse have transformed the practice of business giving. Limit your gifts to items of appropriate value, and you'll demonstrate how much you really value your clients.

TIP 86

Break bread.

Lunch together at your client's convenience in a quiet setting. Ask questions to get your client talking. And be direct when you want to discuss business.

Building a client relationship takes the kind of trust and comfort level not earned solely by the quality of the work you perform. We can dress ourselves up in business suits whenever we wish, but our instincts about people go back to the time when we wore animal skins. Building mutual confidence ultimately requires getting to know each other on a personal level that extends far from the conference table—to a table for two.

It's virtually impossible to say to a client, "Let's get together for an hour or so at your office and just chat." The workplace has been designed and designated for work, even though building a better relationship can enhance your client's productivity and cost efficiency as well build your business. Distractions abound. Sit in a client's office for even ten minutes, and you're likely to be continually interrupted by employees popping in or the phone ringing. What's more, the workplace often defines what *separates* you and your client. Your client's office is *her* territory, not yours. Psychologically, you're always placed a bit on the defensive.

Lunching together can help make clear what bonds the two of you as human beings. As I've mentioned frequently throughout this book, the act of breaking bread together represents a common human endeavor. We all eat. Furthermore, sharing food is a highly social act that implies an element of trust. Much of our tradition of hospitality at home involves offering food to guests. Food also plays a major role in celebrating such milestones as brisses (Jewish ritual circumcisions), christenings, bar mitzvahs, birthdays, and weddings as well as in providing comfort at wakes and funerals. Our most important religious and secular holidays are also built around family meals. Witness the importance of the Thanksgiving turkey.

Lunch makes an outstanding business meal because it takes place during the middle of the day. Not every client responds to the early morning demands of the power breakfast, and dinner keeps people from getting home to their families. Just as important, a restaurant, no matter what its status, serves as a neutral setting that puts you and your client on an equal footing. Ultimately, conducting a business lunch with a client is as simple as, well, eating lunch. Here's all you have to do:

Be flexible. Give your client a choice of days and times to get together. You'll maximize your success if you meet when your client is relaxed rather than rushed by impending meetings or reports. Try to be aware of times when your client may not wish to eat at all. Muslims, for example, fast during the day throughout the month of Ramadan.

Select a restaurant within your means. You don't have to overspend to make the right impression. It's the communication between you and your client, not the show at the restaurant, that counts. Besides, if you spend too much for lunch, you could leave your client wondering whether she's spending too much on your services.

Consider your client's tastes. If you don't know, ask your client about her food preferences. This can spare you from taking a vegetarian to a steak house or finding out that your client never eats Thai food.

Opt for a quiet place. No matter how good the food or how exciting the ambience, a loud restaurant can make it difficult to conduct a conversation. Remember, your goal is to learn more about your client and have your client learn more about you.

Ask questions. Getting to know your client better starts with being an attentive listener. Encourage your client to talk by displaying an interest in her background, hobbies, and work. Keep asking questions to prevent the conversation from running into those awkward silences. And since most people enjoy talking about themselves, you'll make your client feel comfortable with you right away. Most important, you'll often uncover a number of attitudes or preferences that will guide your approach to conducting business with your client in the future.

Be direct about business. Not infrequently you'll want to go beyond social matters and ask your client about a project you're working on, about relationships with other client staff members, or even about a problem that needs resolving. Once you've had the opportunity to chat and see each other as people, not just as client and service provider, you can bring up the matter at hand. A straightforward question is always the simplest, since it lets your client know just what you have on your mind and is least likely to be misinterpreted. It's amazing how quickly complicated problems can get solved in a relaxed environment without interruptions.

Get a receipt. Business lunches are a legitimate expense, even if the amount you can write off is only fractional. If your waiter or waitress hasn't left a credit card or other receipt, ask for one. Then put it away quickly so that your focus remains on your client, not your bookkeeping.

Write a thank-you note. Is it backwards to write a thank-you when you're the one who hosted the lunch? Not at all. You're thanking your client for taking the time from her busy day to join you. Show your clients appreciation every chance you get.

In an increasingly impersonal world, lunch enables people to put a human face on business. Give your clients an opportunity to see you as a person, and you'll give them more reasons to continue doing business with you.

TIP 87

Put friendship in perspective.

Never use friendship to gain business. Separate business and social activities to avoid conflicts. And always recognize a client-friend's business authority.

Some years back, a friend of mine, who had freelanced as a direct mail copywriter, formed a small direct mail ad agency with a partner. From time to time he asked me if I was interested in writing a project for him. I repeatedly declined, explaining that I would rather not have business intrude on our friendship. Through the years, his agency opened offices across the country, then became global in scope. At any time I could have increased my billings handsomely by asking to be included among the freelancers his agency used. But I didn't. Had there ever been a problem, our friendship could have been compromised. And it's much more difficult to make a friend than it is to acquire a client.

However, when several clients of mine became friends over the years, I didn't stop working for them. But I did have to consciously remind myself that I was obligated not to let friendship overwhelm the business side of these relationships. It's often easier to lose clients—and friends—than it is to win them.

Periodically, business and social relationships overlap. You can balance them successfully as long as you remain aware of the pitfalls—and prevent them through common sense:

Establish a friendship free from ulterior motives. You needn't be someone's friend to earn his business. But a friendship based only on an interest in profits is no friendship at all. At some point your client will discover that his friendship is less important to you than he thinks. Then you will not only lose the client but risk burning a bridge behind you and compromising your reputation. Nurture a social relationship only if you enjoy someone's company outside the business realm.

Separate your business and social activities. Friendship simply cannot be governed by the rules that apply to a business agreement. Entering into a social relationship with a client does not suddenly limit your client-friend's options. Always leave him free to do business with whomever he chooses and to leave you out of his business plans whenever he chooses. Adding expectations and jealousy to the mix will inexorably lead to the failure of both the friendship and the business relationship.

Acknowledge your client-friend's authority. When you're working on a project with your friend, view him first and foremost as your client. Remember that decision-making won't be shared as if you were pondering where to play golf or what movie to see. Your client always has the right to say how a project should be undertaken and what standards you should meet.

Be careful when a friend asks you to become a client. The pressures of business can easily rupture a friendship. Your friend may expect more of you than anyone can reasonably deliver—as if you didn't give every project for every client a 100 percent effort. From your friend's perspective, any problems with your solution can quickly change from business to personal. Conversely, if your friend isn't satisfied with your work, the matter tends to become much more personal and emotional for you. After all, you *expect* him to like your work *out of friendship.* Business judgments must remain objective. If your feelings tend to be fragile, don't expose them.

Charge reasonable fees to friends. Not infrequently, friends will call on your services because they believe they'll get a deal. You may wish to give a friend a discount if it's possible, but no friend has the right to anticipate that you'll give your services away. You have only so much time in which to earn a living. Unfair expectations can drive a wedge between the two of you. Be clear and firm about the services you provide, the way you work, and the fees you must charge.

Keep friendship in its proper place, and you'll keep your business free from unnecessary entanglements.

TIP 88

Practice tolerance.

Accept the fact that your clients are only human. Learn to live with their foibles to prevent needless antagonism and loss of business.

When Seth, my eldest, was a small boy, he would not eat any food that had been mixed with another food on his plate. Peas had better not intrude into the mashed potatoes. Potatoes touching his chicken? Unthinkable! A carrot stick leaning over a hamburger? New plate, please! Whatever the reasons for such behavior—and many small children seem to share that distaste for mixing—we continued to love Seth. And, reasoning that we would encounter more important issues in the years to come, we managed to keep the different foods on his plate as separate as possible. Parents learn to live with these things.

Adults though they may be, clients have their own likes and dislikes. The client with whom I have had the longest-standing relationship—approximately sixteen years—has a sense of humor that is completely different from my own. He takes a droll midwestern approach compared to my New York attitude: "Funny? I'll tell you what's funny!" The gap in our comedic outlooks would be relatively unimportant in most fields, but it often proved challenging whenever he asked me to write a humorous radio commercial for him. To me, the finished scripts and produced commercials never seemed funny. Not even whimsical. *Nada.* But I nonetheless always wrote the kind of commercial he wanted while providing alternate versions I *knew* were funny. I valued his business and respected his right to set parameters for the work he paid me to do.

The manager of the marketing department at a major corporate client of mine hates photographs of hands. To me, hands are fascinating and wonderfully expressive. To her, they're body parts. Once I learned her rules, I stopped suggesting hands as artwork for brochures or mailers, even when I knew they would be very effective. I still work for her department and am delighted to do so. Her preferences, not my ego, dictate the direction of every project she pays me to do.

To achieve mastery of your core skills, you must believe in your own judgment. But to make the *business* of freelancing work, you must maintain your client relationships in spite of some fundamental differences. Obviously, disagreements over the basics can become real impediments (see Tip 89). Most, however, simply require that you take a deep breath, count to ten, smile, and say, "Okay, I hear you." Because your livelihood is at stake and ours is an imperfect world, remember these points:

Your job is to please your client. Your client pays you to advance her interests, not yours. She always retains the right to set the goals for her business and to approve the solutions that affect it.

Clients have final authority. Naturally, you owe your clients your best recommendations and efforts, never simply "what the client wants to hear." But once you've made a proposal or presented a solution, concede your client her right to choose. Defend your ideas by all means, but once you've done so, defer to her. Business relationships are neither democratic nor open-ended.

Client budgets are often limited. It's easy to spend other people's money. But when we shop for ourselves, we're as likely to go to a discount store as a top-of-the-line boutique. Clients may not always budget adequately to attain the quality they demand or should achieve. But the ability to work within a budget and still produce satisfactory results is truly what separates outstanding freelancers from egotists who eventually fall by the wayside.

Clients deserve alternate solutions. You want your client to jump up and down with joy at the first idea or solution you present. Unfortunately, clients don't always know what they want—or should want. Ask your client to tell you specifically what she doesn't like about your solution—and what she does like, too. Keep her talking until she expresses herself clearly. Sometimes the solution to a problem is relatively simple (see Tip 63). Then use her critique to formulate a new solution. If you've made headway, you can probably finish the project quickly. If you're still stuck, determine whether your agreed-upon fee will still cover your time. If not, negotiate an additional fee to keep working. At all times remember that most service-oriented solutions are subjective in part or in whole. If your client is willing to keep hiring you and paying you, even when she seems to be less than wildly enthusiastic, take it as a vote of confidence. You're providing what *she* wants. Or see Tip 89.

Clients don't have to be friends. A client's personal habits or personality may not be to your liking. Some people are brusque even with family and friends, so you as a freelancer may never see their bright side—if they have one. But if your client is honest, competent, and reasonably considerate, you can look for warmth elsewhere (see Tip 87).

Clients appreciate even-tempered service providers with common sense and a willingness to stay focused on their business needs. Thicken your hide and thin out your ego, and you'll fatten your wallet.

TIP 89

Know when to say when.

Terminate clients who are abusive, rude, dissatisfied, or dishonest. Sacrifice short-term gain for long-term growth and peace of mind.

Oh, the clients I would love to have told off when I was an employee! Like the egomaniac in San Antonio who couldn't put three words together to total more than four syllables yet made life so miserable for my bosses and coworkers. Or the martinet in Los Angeles whose wife knew nothing about the product but reviewed all the ads and vetoed them if they contained a color she hated. Not to mention the tantrum-thrower in San Francisco who believed that making an easily rectifiable mistake was tantamount to betraying the flag.

I always thought that the ultimate joy of freelancing would be the opportunity to tell a client where to go or simply to leave him twisting in the wind. Once you assume responsibility for running your own business, however, fantasy quickly yields to reality. Faced with another mortgage payment and a bill from the orthodontist, you become amazingly willing to go the extra mile to keep a client. Yet if you go *beyond* that extra mile with a truly impossible client, you risk ruin. Bad clients are bad business. That's why I've walked away from a few.

Over a period of years, I wrote a variety of materials, including a book, for an interior designer. She was a lovely woman, but one who constantly needed someone to hold her hand. Her life always seemed just too frantic. Consequently she frequently left me waiting at her office when I had arrived on time for a meeting—not conducive to maintaining goodwill when I had to drive an hour each way. Sometimes she simply wasn't there at all. And then she started panicking over my very modest fees. I said good-bye.

Over time, a couple of ad agencies with whom I'd had good relationships became casual about my payments. Of course, the presidents of both outfits continued to drive expensive foreign cars and live consumer-oriented lifestyles, perhaps made possible in some small part by the interest they earned on the funds they owed to me. I collected my fees, then burned rubber.

Keep working for a bad client, and you can only lose—time, money, self-esteem, and your standing in your business community. Cutting the strings is your best investment when a client demonstrates any of the following:

Abusiveness. No client is entitled to scream at you or call you names. And when a client does so to employees or others, you're listening to a strong clue that sooner or later he's going to try to bully or take advantage of you—and you'll be left the loser.

Disregard for your time. Business can get hectic, and clients can be delayed. But when a client continually keeps you waiting for meetings or fails to show up, you're dealing with someone who holds you worthless both as a service provider and as a person. Sooner or later that attitude will produce other symptoms unhealthy for your business.

Inaccuracy or untruthfulness. To successfully undertake a project, you must have sound information. Whenever you're misinformed by a client, your work, of necessity, shoots wide of the target. When a client cannot provide you with the facts and details you need, or when he denies responsibility for leading you in the wrong direction, *you* will be made the scapegoat.

Continual dissatisfaction. Some people never seem to be pleased. A client may continually express displeasure with your work, causing projects to drag on and leaving you to invest more time than you'll be paid for—when you get paid. Sooner rather than later that client will withhold payment for a substantial amount of work you've done, or he'll tell others that you are not very good at what you do.

Possessiveness. You may feel flattered that a client wants you all to himself. But unless his projects are wildly profitable for you or unless he's prepared to pay for an exclusive agreement (see Tip 48), he has no right to suggest or insist that you give up working for his competitors. Call it blackmail. Call it restraint of trade. Whatever you call it, limiting your availability in the marketplace can have negative consequences when your freelance competitors make inroads at potential clients you need to expand your business.

Avoidance of fiscal responsibility. You prepare estimates to help your client budget effectively and control the work done on a project. To avoid later disagreements it is imperative that your client sign each estimate before you start working (see Tip 49). It's equally important that your client pay you on time when work has been completed (see Tips 54–58). Lack of response in these areas can doom you to major financial losses.

Continual unhappiness with your fees. No client is obligated to agree to any fee he feels is too high, just as you're not obligated to work for a fee you believe to be too low. So you negotiate each fee, come to an agreement, and put that aspect of the project behind you (see Tips 43 and 44). When your client keeps complaining about your fees after the fact, he's really communicating that he doesn't trust you, value your work, or see a future in your relationship. Sooner or later he's going to surprise you by withholding payment or giving projects you expect to do to others.

Never give up a client without thinking the matter through, thinking again, and weighing the effects on your business with total objectivity. But when a client becomes an impediment to the smooth functioning of your business by taking time from your other clients' projects, or when he causes you real emotional or financial distress, you have more than a right to terminate him—you have an obligation. Maintain a sense of joy and contentment in your client relationships, and you'll maintain your long-term growth and success.

TIP 90

Leave your bridges standing.

Accept the end of a client relationship by concluding it on as pleasant a note as possible to preserve the option for a future association and to avoid damaging rumors.

For a number of years I did quite a bit of work with a graphic designer whom I considered to be quite a rarity. He was not only an immensely talented designer but a shrewd and disciplined marketing thinker as well. Our relationship was excellent. We respected each other's work and spent considerable time talking about business and life in general. I learned quite a bit from him and valued our relationship personally as well as professionally. And then he dropped me.

I had sent him an estimate for a number of related projects we were going to do together for an area hospital. I kept my fees modest, since I understood the client's budget constraints. Seemingly out of the blue, the designer told me that another writer—who had apparently underbid me—would be doing the work. Okay, I thought, he's under pressure from the client. Fair enough. We'll do the next project together. So I called periodically. He never answered. I sent mailers. No response. Then, a year or so later, he called and asked me to write a press release for a client and send it to New York. He had a twenty-four-hour deadline and was leaving town, so he would trust me to follow through without him. Why hadn't he called his other writer? Because the fellow, though very creative, was not dependable and was frequently late with work. This job had to be done right and on time. Figuring that the designer had learned his lesson, I wrote the release and FedExed it to New York. I got paid without delay. But I didn't hear from him again for years in spite of dozens of phone calls, mailers, and holiday cards—until I received a card inviting me to a retrospective of his work.

In time, some of your clients will terminate relationships, and you will conclude others. The client life cycle, like life itself, is always finite. I remember, for example, *Advertising Age* reporting that Delta Air Lines was considering splitting up its $100 million account after fifty-one years with the same agency. To help you keep your emotions balanced, remember that client relationships can end for any number of reasons:

Clients get bored. As unfair or silly as it may seem, clients often get tired of working with the same freelancers, no matter how outstanding they are. They cast loyalty aside to see if the grass is really greener. Sometimes they think they can get better work. Sometimes they think they can save money. Sometimes they just don't think at all. But they always have the right to select whomever they want.

Client contacts move on. You build relationships with people, not companies. Your individual client may get a promotion—or a pink slip. Either way, her replacement may not know you or wish to inherit you, choosing instead to build her own power base with freelancers who are loyal to her and her way of thinking. Some clients leave town. Others retire and take your relationship with them into their golden years. New mothers and occasionally new fathers leave work to care for their families. And a number of clients go out on their own to freelance as you do.

Client budgets shrink. You can control the quality of the work you do but not the quantity of work your client needs. Even as the American economy soars in the nineties, budgets often shrink or disappear altogether.

Competitors outmuscle you. As hard as you work, a competitor may increase her business at your expense. I've pushed aside a lot of competitors in my time. A few have eventually taken business away from me. Every businessperson shares this experience. The saying "you can't win 'em all" definitely applies. Triumph and defeat are two sides of the same coin.

There are times when you can't do a thing to retain a client, even when the relationship seems to have been very positive. But you always have a choice regarding how you react to the end of a relationship. Your response can have a profound effect on your business over the years that follow. It's always in your best interest to take certain measures:

Cast aside guilt. Don't automatically blame yourself when a client shows you the door or simply melts away. No freelancer can exert total control over any—let alone every—situation. You're in business for the long haul, and letting your emotional gas tank drain down to empty will have a negative impact on your business. As the Eagles sing, "Get over it!"

Sound a wake-up call. Forget the guilt, but remember to evaluate the relationship to determine how you might have done a better job. Turn the shock of losing a client, for whatever reason, into an opportunity to take stock of your business practices and goals. You'll strengthen your existing relationships and build an even more solid foundation for new clients.

Free your client from blame. A client may end your relationship for any number of reasons—financial, personal, or irrational. Although you may believe that a client's reasons are not justified, you would be foolish to do any more than express your regret that the relationship will not continue and accept your client's right to move on. To protect your own best interests, it's important that you take the next two suggestions to heart.

Be graceful. Don't say or do anything that reflects negatively on your ex-client. Even if your client is at fault, making a lot of noise can lead others to see you as vindictive and conclude that your client was right to let you go. It's perfectly acceptable to calmly express your disappointment, but leave it at that.

Be gracious. If your parting is at all amicable, even if you are rejected for a competitor, thank your client for the relationship you've had. Remember, no client is ever obligated to give you business. Gratitude is always appropriate.

Why not just burn your bridges in a fit of self-righteous glory? Because change works both ways. Clients whose budgets shrink may suddenly gain new funding as their businesses evolve. A client contact at one company may show you the door, then show up at another company and need your services. The competitor who seems so attractive today may prove to be inadequate tomorrow. And the grapevine that passes along your name to other clients will praise or damn you without fully understanding your motivations. It's not enough to *be* right. You have to *appear* to be right.

Take the rise and fall of client relationships in stride and take a positive approach to each concluding relationship. Understanding and self-control will take your business toward new opportunities.

Chapter 11

TEAMING UP WITH ASSOCIATES

Once, I took a walking tour of an ancient Roman temple dedicated to the Egyptian goddess Isis. I was free to wander around the inner courtyard and some of the rooms. Wherever I turned, I saw graceful columns and colorful frescoes. Most remarkably, I was in San Francisco's De Young Museum while the temple remained in Italy. Thanks to a special helmet, a control pad, and a very powerful computer, my son Aaron and I enjoyed our visit to the past through virtual reality.

The new economic age has also fostered the virtual company. As Hedrick Smith writes in *Rethinking America,* "Size and scale, advantages long enjoyed by America, are now often liabilities, less desirable in the new competitive arena." With considerable frequency, individuals and groups from various enterprises form units to pursue a specific goal. When the task has been completed, they form new units. Within companies, hierarchies frequently have been flattened dramatically while rigid tables of organizations have given way to work groups that continually grow, shrink, and change as one project is completed and another undertaken.

Technology has helped make the virtual company, or work group, function. With everyone able to communicate with everyone else through computer networks, E-mail, intranets, and the

Internet—even across the globe—work groups can take advantage of their unprecedented flexibility to put the right people together wherever they may be, and they can also take advantage of economies of scale. Need a team of five to handle a project? No problem. Need a hundred people? No problem, either.

What does this have to do with freelancers? A lot. While we, by definition, prefer to exist as one-person business entities, it's generally more profitable not to work alone. Moreover, freelancers have very much played a role in pioneering the concept of the flexible work group, teaming up with other freelancers, and sometimes with clients, to help create virtual "enterprises" focused on a single project for only the duration of that project.

Working as part of a team doesn't diminish the spirit of freelancing. It enhances it by providing additional opportunities. But, as always, you have to select your teammates and carefully structure responsibilities to turn opportunities into profits.

The following tips will guide you in finding your way through virtual work groups and show you how to expand your business by taking part in projects that require more than what you can provide on your own.

TIP 91

Coordinate and subordinate.

Avoid duplication of skills, respect your associates' opinions, share the pie, and free each other from obligations when the job is completed.

Three days before I began this tip, I formed a work group partnership with two associates. A major Bay Area amusement park planned to mail information to the human resources directors of three hundred large companies soliciting their corporate picnics. Of course, I would provide creative direction and copywriting for the project. But I'm not an art director or a computer production artist. So I brought in a designer I've teamed up with for several years. Neither of us gets involved in printing or mail house work, so we brought in a vendor who could handle that aspect. What we established was a virtual direct mail advertising agency—for one project. We signed no contracts and created no legal entities. We simply specified our tasks and agreed to bill the client separately.

I've probably been involved in virtual agencies since I started freelancing. Often a client will ask me if I know a designer. I know several. The designers I team up with are sometimes asked to provide writers. They call me. When I used to create jingles for radio, I called in one of several music producers. Any time a project required multiple skills, a new team would be formed.

But freelance teams needn't restrict themselves to only responding to client requests. One freelance art director and I actively solicit business by calling prospects and sending out promotional mailings and novelties. New clients often believe that the art director and I are a single company. We're not. We estimate and bill jobs separately, though we coordinate our efforts to save clients' time. What's more, I've sat in on dozens of presentations by small ad agencies as a member of their creative teams, which I was, though I remained a freelancer.

Informal partnerships can be highly profitable since they provide entrée to projects that a freelancer acting alone would often have to pass up. But these partnerships work only when you and your associates . . .

Complement each other. Duplication of skills makes no sense unless a specific task is too great for one individual. When two or more people must bring the same skills to a project, it's critical to avoid duplication of *roles.* Each individual should be assigned a clearly distinct role no matter how closely their tasks are related.

Control your egos. If a camel is a horse put together by committee, what does that say about committees? Each associate is entitled to a say about how the project will be handled strategically and what standards will be adhered to in order to produce quality work. But unless each member is willing to yield to others, a project is doomed. (For a discussion of leadership and role assignments, see Tip 92.)

Arrive at mutually acceptable fees. Workloads may differ in a project, with some team members required to do more than others. Furthermore, individual associates may have wildly varying fee structures. If your fees are relatively high, you risk arousing envy and ultimately creating stumbling blocks if you make significantly more money than someone who performs the same quantity of work—or more. Likewise, you may resent someone charging a fee that's substantially higher than yours for doing considerably less work only because her fee structure is far above your own. The solution? First be sure that total team fees and expenses fall within your client's budget. Then split the fee portion as evenly as possible, taking into account the degrees of responsibility involved. Projects flow smoothly only when all members feel they are sharing equitably in the rewards. A more highly paid freelancer makes a sensible investment when she lowers her fee to foster team harmony, the success of a project, and repeat business—the truly key source of long-term profitability.

Respect each other's individuality and freedom. The virtual team exists once and once only. When a project is completed, so are the associates' obligations to each other. Good working relationships will encourage repeated associations, but the formation of a team for one project should not be seen as obligating any of the parties. Freelancers are, by their very nature, free to choose their own paths. Also, a client may be highly pleased with one team member and dissatisfied with another. The team member who has found favor may be asked to bring a different associate into another project and should be free to do so without feeling guilty or facing recrimination.

Freelancing and working well with others go hand in hand. Guide your associations with care and thought, and you can guide your business to the next level.

TIP 92

Identify the alpha member.

Select a team leader to provide key client contact, oversee the budget, set schedules, and help move the project to completion.

Wolves travel in packs. Like many other species, they work well together and depend on one another for survival. To maximize their efficiency, they establish a pecking order. The leader, the toughest and perhaps shrewdest, is known as the alpha male. Teamwork among humans isn't much different. The *key* to group success lies in leadership—male or female. When you put a group of associates together, someone must take overall responsibility for each project.

No individual can assume that someone else will do whatever is necessary. Since a team of two or more associates creates a virtual company, you must work out with your associates who will provide each of the following:

Project leadership. Clients easily get confused when they have to speak with more than one person regarding a project's progress—and risk getting more than one answer to a question. Select a team leader to serve as the key client contact, to finalize budgets and schedules, and to manage the project through completion. If you have an ongoing association with someone, you can take turns doing this, depending on who your client is and whose additional workload may or may not preclude team leadership at the time. As an option, you can roll over contact from phase to phase. Working with a designer, I will usually organize our approach to the client, then deal with the client through the development of creative concepts and initial copy. Once the client sees the actual design, the designer will generally take over client contact, since most of the work at that point involves her expertise.

Quality control. Someone must be empowered to make decisions and have the final word about the quality of the project and how it is to be presented.

Payment. If you are being paid with a single check, the team leader must follow through to be sure payment is made and funds are distributed. This generally mandates issuing IRS Form 1099s during January of the following calendar year (see Tip 95). If you are being paid separately, the team leader must check to see that all associates have been paid, even if they sent invoices at different times. Associates are responsible for their own payment but should alert each other when a problem exists to help keep a client from taking advantage of any individual.

New business. You and your associates don't have to wait for clients to knock on your door. You can divide new-business responsibilities, then individually develop contacts for your virtual company. Make calls. Send out mailers. Follow up. Arrange presentations. Often the solicitor becomes the alpha member on projects that he or she brings in unless you have a standing arrangement with which everyone is comfortable.

Organize your virtual company by dividing roles from the top down, and you'll see your business opportunities multiply.

TIP 93

Follow the manual.

Put client information, budgets, and schedules in writing. Then follow up with memos to make sure every associate is on the same page.

Anyone who has ever served in the army knows that there are three ways to perform any task—the right way, the wrong way, and the army way. The right way is often dictated by common sense and sometimes revealed by the experiences of buddies. The wrong way becomes evident when your platoon sergeant finds reasons for you to drop and do twenty push-ups. The army way requires no guesswork at all. It is clearly expressed in a never-ending flow of printed manuals that break every function—from firing an assault rifle to brushing your teeth—into discrete, concrete steps: "Do it like this and only like this."

Organization—keeping track of budgets and schedules along with maintaining communication—can make all the difference between success and failure. If you work by yourself, you have total control. It's easy to think of whatever works for you as an individual as the right way. When you succeed, it's because of your own efforts. Fail at something, and the wrong way becomes apparent. Your client will willingly play the role of platoon sergeant, leaving you to ruminate over what you've done—or failed to do—and determine the improvements you need to make.

Work with others, however, and there's only one way to ensure your team's success—"the army way." This doesn't involve lengthy manuals and rigid procedures but rather a formalized approach to keeping a group project running smoothly. It's easy to assume that your associates will be as organized and conscientious as you are and that details will be attended to even when no one has mentioned them. It's just as easy to fall on your face when your assumptions prove wrong. When two or more people team up, working without clearly stated guidelines becomes a major liability. A virtual company needs not only a real leader but a real structure for doing business. To ensure the success of any team project:

Commit business processes to paper. Ever play telephone? One person whispers a word or phrase into another's ear. The second person whispers to a third, and so on. What the last person says usually bears little resemblance to what the first person said. Oral instructions and reminders tend to be misunderstood or forgotten. Keep a project file in your computer with all the important information you need and back it up with hard copies.

Write organizational memos. Most people hate writing memos and reading them. But successful businesspeople—from freelancers to executives of major corporations—understand that everyone involved in a project must be fully informed in writing. Just as huskies can't pull a sled unless they all run in the same direction, team members can't undertake their tasks and gauge their progress without the same information presented in the same format. Start everyone off on an equal footing with a concise memo specifying the nature of the project, its parameters, its goals, and the requirements of each associate. (For more about memos, see Tip 65.)

Create a detailed budget. When your client gives you a budget figure, break it down into every possible component covering associates' fees and project expenses. If the budget will not be sufficient, discuss the shortfall with all associates to determine whether fees can be reduced or alternative methods for completing the project can be developed. If the budget still falls short, present an alternative to your client and cite the reasons more money will be necessary. When your client asks you to suggest a budget, take the same care in order to bid competitively. Paying attention to detail will not only impress your client but help you control costs once you undertake the project.

Set a schedule. Planning a project is like driving across the country. You need a road map and a sense of timing to get from one point to another within a given time frame. Break your project down into each of the steps associates will be required to take—from gathering client input and background information through brainstorming, preliminary concepts, detailed follow-through, and revisions—and establish dates by which these steps will be completed.

Write and distribute update memos. Every associate should receive your organizational memo, budget, and schedule. When the project is under way, periodically send memos notifying associates—*and your client*—when key activities have been completed or changes agreed upon. By putting information in writing, you communicate it uniformly and you protect yourself against accusations that instructions were never clearly given.

Formalize client approval. If assumptions among associates are dangerous, any assumption made about a client can be suicidal. Keeping clients informed with memos is just the start. Whatever your project, get your client to sign or initial your copy, layout, design, report, proof, or code. This will protect you both from claims that the project was not completed to your client's satisfaction (a not uncommon practice when a client's supervisor or family member expresses disapproval after the fact) but also from financial liability if a client suddenly discovers he doesn't like a photo, color, graph, or detail when the solution goes into physical production.

There is nothing casual about successful freelancing, even when you have sole responsibility for a project. When you work with associates, the need to formalize your business processes grows exponentially along with the risk of misunderstandings, recriminations, and financial loss. Go by the book to secure a team project's success, and your books will reflect increased earnings.

TIP 94

Make maintenance routine.

Form relationships with a variety of associates, share fees and responsibilities enthusiastically, and develop potential relationships before they're needed.

Polygamy may be illegal in the United States, but multiple relationships with associates who complement your skills and abilities can be crucial to achieving your financial goals. Over the years I've had the opportunity to team up with a number of freelancers, including designers, music producers, and micro ad agencies. Generally, I conducted several such relationships at the same time.

What's wrong with monogamy in your business? No single individual can always meet every criterion relating to every project with which you need assistance. Look at each potential associate as a unique resource who can bring special skills and abilities to a specific task. Determine who is right for the job by evaluating the style of each person's work, the level of his fees, his ability to work within a given budget, his knowledge of the special field or discipline the project encompasses, and, when necessary, the likelihood that he will relate to your client.

Likewise, expect that your associates will have a clear understanding of how those factors apply to you when they seek assistance on a project—and leave them equally free to choose other freelancers as needed.

Because associations can often be as important to your business as clients, you'll want to do the following:

Maintain multiple relationships. Team up with as many associates as you can to maximize the resources available for servicing your clients and to increase the amount of work others offer you. You can increase your opportunities by establishing relationships with associates in at least three areas:

- *Different geographic locations.* Associates' clients may be geographically based, giving you greater access to the total market and avoiding hurt feelings over perceived conflicts.
- *Different industries.* You can broaden your client base horizontally while acquiring valuable additional knowledge and problem-solving capabilities.
- *Different disciplines.* You will apply your skills to a greater variety of challenges—for example, designing ads with one associate and brochures with another, or planning corporate

picnics for an associate in the business world and organizing festive wedding celebrations for another who deals with private individuals.

Maintain goodwill. Display your sense of teamwork in sharing fees equitably, fulfilling all your responsibilities, and being calm and considerate when deadlines and other pressures raise the tension level. The day I outlined this tip, an associate who runs a micro ad agency with her husband called me to write a direct mail package *that afternoon.* Their largest client—with whom we had worked together frequently—had procrastinated only to face a very imminent deadline. I put aside work on several other tasks and completed the project within hours. The next day, my associate called to say that the client was very happy (making the agency a hero), but that the budget was far too small to cover our normal fees. Knowing the value of the client to the agency and the value of the association to me, I gave her carte blanche to reduce my fee to whatever level was necessary to provide the agency with a reasonable return. We'd shared when profits were high, and we would share reduced fees when helping the client through a tight spot was in our long-term interest.

Maintain a roster of potential associates. Stay aloof from others in your field, and you risk not being able to bring needed resources to a project; you might have to call in someone you don't know and take your chances that everything will work out. Check the Yellow Pages, read trade magazines (particularly the classified ads, where many freelancers advertise), and ask people you know to recommend talented people in your field. Call potential associates from time to time, ask for their résumés and samples of their work, and meet with those who seem promising. You'll then be able to respond quickly and confidently when a client asks you to coordinate functions you can't perform by yourself.

Mutually satisfying relationships can open doors to outstanding new opportunities. By promoting the interests of a variety of associates, you'll be promoting your own success.

TIP 95

Study the understudy conundrum.

Balance the advantages that hiring subcontractors can have on your profits against the risks of losing clients to people who actually do the work.

Americans love underdogs. So it was only natural that Hollywood musicals of the thirties and forties sometimes featured the theme of the chorus girl who becomes an overnight sensation. In movies like *42nd Street,* a Broadway star is unable to go on, setting the stage—figuratively and literally—for the debut of a small-town chorine with stars in her eyes who happens to be able to sing and dance and who knows all the lines to the show. The cast and crew rally around the heroine who conquers the jaded but warm hearts of the denizens of the Great White Way, thrills the panicked producers, and still endears herself to one and all with her humility.

Understudies can be saviors or conquerors, depending upon their talent and visibility. Few people know that baseball great Lou Gehrig's former record of playing in 2,130 consecutive games came at the expense of Wally Pipp, who sat out a game with a headache and never returned to the New York Yankees' lineup.

Subcontracting work can be tempting because you can:

Avoid passing up projects when you're busy. You simply pay your sub part of your fee to do most of the work.

Generate starter and alternative ideas. Too busy to get a project moving without some momentum? Your sub can provide concepts from which you can select and develop.

Take advantage of specialized knowledge. No one knows everything. By choosing a sub with expertise you don't have, you can manage the project while the sub makes it work.

A friend of mine spent some years freelancing between working as a copywriter for ad agencies and forming his own immensely successful agency. From time to time, when his workload grew too heavy and he didn't want to sacrifice income, he called in other writers to handle projects for him. His subcontractors had little or no contact with his clients. In that way he protected his hard-won business. On the other hand, his subs received all their information secondhand, and there are times when getting the word directly from a client can make a major difference in a project's success.

I've occasionally thought about hiring subs, but I've never done so. I don't oppose it on principle. But I have come to believe that clients who call me do so expressly because they want *me* to do the work. I'm also aware that no arrangement is perfect, as Hollywood and baseball have indicated. So you, as a freelancer, have to weigh the risks of subcontracting against the rewards. Consider the downside:

Supervision. You must spend enough time guiding your sub in doing the job correctly. You must also take the time to see that the job is executed in your style; otherwise you risk giving away the fact that you were hired but did not do the work. This can end a client relationship quickly.

Quality. Every project you complete must meet *your* standards. If your sub can't do the job as you want it done, you'll have to do it yourself and lose money in the process. Of course, you can seek to hire a sub who is better than you, but you may be hard-pressed to negotiate a fee that will satisfy both of you.

Communication. To make a project work, you must keep your sub informed. But you face a major hazard when you take your sub with you to a client meeting. Following your introduction, an unprincipled sub can contact your client and reveal that she did the work in order to take the relationship from you. This happens with great frequency. I would never compromise any of my ad agency clients, for whom I am, in effect, subbing, even though I have frequent contact with their clients. But I definitely understand the paranoia some of them exhibit when, at a critical time, a visit to the client or telephone contact is called for.

Bear in mind that if you do hire a sub who is not incorporated, you must file an IRS Form 1099A (miscellaneous income) if you paid that sub total fees of $600 or more in a calendar year. You send the 1099 to your sub in January of the year following that in which payment was made. You also send the IRS their copy of the 1099 along with a Form 1096 transmittal letter. If you fail to file appropriate 1099s and are audited, expect to pay a costly fine.

To subcontract or not to subcontract? That is the question. Follow Polonius's words in *Hamlet,* "To thine own self be true," and you will find the answer that is true to your sense of what is best for your business.

TIP 96

Know your role at the masquerade.

Understand the limits imposed by a company or freelancer who hires you as a subcontractor, and consider your client's clients off-limits.

Based on experience, I often equate good freelancers with chameleons. I've appeared at numerous meetings as part of some ad agency's staff, although I always remained a freelancer. Over the years my name has been printed on at least a dozen agency business cards with titles ranging from copywriter to creative director—or with no title at all. Periodically I've been listed on the staff rosters of two, three, and four agencies at the same time.

This involves a bit of a masquerade but one that has never adversely affected a client. While some agencies make it known to their clients that I'm a freelancer, others fear that their clients will be put off by their lack of a formally contracted staff. Frankly, my being a freelancer makes no difference to the quality of the work the agencies do. My agency clients and I form a virtual partnership (see the introduction to this chapter), and several of my relationships with agencies go back many years and are longer than those they've had with most of their permanent employees. I know each agency, its clients, its style of doing business, and the ways in which they want me to assist them. It works.

Masquerading can work for you as well. If you fulfill a role as a subcontractor or virtual team member under someone else's leadership, however, you must bear several responsibilities:

Defer to your client. Let the person who hires you take the lead and set the parameters of what you will be doing and how you'll do it. As your relationship lengthens and deepens, you may earn a significant degree of independence. Nonetheless, you must always remember who signs your checks.

Refrain from communicating with the person to whom your client reports. Unless you have been given specific permission, direct contact is taboo. If firsthand communication seems necessary—and often it will—ask your client if you can call, fax, E-mail or even visit. If your client prefers to handle all communications, accept that decision as imperfect but within your client's rights.

Respect your client's fears. No matter how good your relationship, your client will want to limit your contact with his clients and minimize your role in projects. This is only natural (see Tip 95). Don't take it personally, and don't let it spoil your relationship. My agency clients actually serve as my agents and make my life easier by finding business for me. I will do everything I can to represent their best interests.

Never—ever—approach a client's client while your team relationship exists. Maybe you can do the job better or cheaper or both. But if you try to cut your client out of the picture, you will sever the relationship, risk having your reputation trammeled, and violate sound business ethics (see "A Little Extra Advice," following Tip 100). Once broken, trust is very difficult to restore. If your relationship ends, allow some time to pass before targeting the client to avoid being perceived as a poacher. Word travels fast in any industry, and what goes around definitely comes around.

Be willing to be invisible when someone subcontracts your services, and you'll see visible results when you total your billings at year's end.

TIP 97

Examine the harness.

Carefully consider entering into a formal partnership. Give any such arrangement the same thought you would a marriage.

Somewhere in America, Ralph and Alice Kramden are still fighting—and making up, only to fight again. Back in the fifties *The Honeymooners* was a great success on TV. It still runs in syndication and deservedly so. I'm continually entertained by the outrageous bluster of Ralph (Jackie Gleason), and the steely-calm composure of Alice (Audrey Meadows). Not to mention the physical comedy of Art Carney as sidekick Ed Norton. Carney's work alone deserves to be seen by generations to come.

The Kramdens are a wake-up call to those who believe that eternal wedded bliss is effortless. Two people united into one legal entity have to learn to live together in spite of their faults and shortcomings—and we all have those. It's no easier in business. Before you decide that forming a company with a partner will enhance your success, you have several pros and cons to consider.

On the upside:

Two heads are often better than one. If each partner brings different skills to the match, and you both agree on clearly defined individual responsibilities, you can complement each other and create a partnership stronger than each of you individually. Further, your partner may have experience that you lack. Someone who has been in your business longer or has worked with different clients can offer you an opportunity to learn and grow as well as to take advantage of contacts you might otherwise not reach.

Two can live as cheaply as one—sort of. By combining your resources you may be able to afford bigger and better office space, plus the equipment you need to stay competitive. For example, two partners need only one printer, one photocopy machine, one fax machine, and one coffeemaker.

You may be able to win bigger clients and more of them. A partnership that functions correctly can provide more services within the scope of a single project. And because you're partners, you're always there for each other, so you don't have to worry about finding an associate to team up with, particularly on short notice.

You might even buy a little extra time. You need a day off. Maybe two wrapped around a weekend to create a mini-vacation. Or even a regular vacation! It could happen, since your partner will be there to answer the phone, service clients, and complete projects as necessary.

As a freelancer I don't denigrate partnerships at all. But I do suggest that you be aware of the downside:

Someone will lose the power struggle. No matter how you structure the partnership, one of you has to have the final word if you are to function efficiently. Some partners meet this challenge by alternating the presidency of their company each year. But that can pose a problem when one partner believes that she knows more than the other.

Envy can easily erupt. It's no small matter when one partner is responsible for more billings than the other and expects to call the shots—but happens to be wrong about a critical matter. Even when the relationship is a good one, the partner with smaller billings may feel awkward. Or one partner may feel he isn't getting enough credit for the company's success or is taking too much blame for its failures.

Personalities may come apart under fire. This is an old story. When things go well, everyone's happy. When challenges emerge, one or both partners may yield to the pressure and become extremely difficult to live with. It's easy to paint a rosy picture of the future when you're first discussing your new company, but you have to know a potential partner well to be reasonably confident that she won't crack when times turn tough.

Significant others may enter the relationship. Multiply one marriage by three, and you have some potentially scary dynamics. Husbands and wives have been known to "protect" their spouses' interests when they suspect that the other partner isn't living up to his responsibilities or giving their spouse his due. Also, it's not a reach to say that spouses who don't get along can nudge their personal disagreements into the business and make the partners' relationship more difficult.

Having never entered into a formal partnership, I'll hold off on giving specific advice. But I would certainly suggest that you entertain thoughts of partnership carefully, come to know a proposed partner nearly as well as you know yourself, and commit to writing all the details of the partnership—including roles and responsibilities, short- and long-term goals, and remuneration—before you commit.

Consider going into business with someone *at least* as seriously as you would consider marriage, and your decision will go in the right direction.

Chapter 12

EVALUATING SUCCESS

When I was in my twenties I appreciated money but never thought much about possessing it. During two consecutive summer vacations from college, I earned fifty dollars a week—the minimum wage of $1.50 an hour—selling souvenirs at the 1964 New York World's Fair in Queens and then office clerking for *Family Weekly* magazine in Manhattan. My first job after college was as an army basic trainee earning $94 a month. When I arrived at officer candidate school and started making $200 a month, I had no idea what to do with all that money. Two years later, as a first lieutenant, I was taking home $512 a month, housing allowance included. Then backward I went, pulling in a tidy $450 monthly for teaching English at a private school.

Money isn't everything. Each of my summer jobs, after years as a camper, camp waiter, and counselor, gave me a new perspective on the working world. Then, in the army, I learned far more about people—and myself—than I'd known before. And later on, teaching proved enjoyable and a wonderful way to begin my marriage, since our apartment was only a ten-minute walk from the campus, and Carolyn and I had time off together during winter and spring vacations.

My first job in advertising was low-paying as well—another $450 a month. I was a financial underachiever, but I really couldn't wait to get to work each day. I'd discovered something I really liked to do, and I believed that, in time, my financial reward, like water, would reach its natural level.

Some freelancers discover that only by working on their own can they maximize their income. Others give up a great deal of money in exchange for nonmonetary rewards. In truth, there is no one way to measure success. Read Tips 98 and 99, and I think you'll be able to identify the features that make your individual assessment of freelancing valid.

TIP 98

Eagle-eye the metrics.

Examine your income objectively to determine whether you're meeting your financial goals now and where your future earnings are headed.

Everyone knows that money can't buy happiness. But as Tevye says in *Fiddler on the Roof*, "It's no shame to be poor. But it's no great honor, either." There are several ways to evaluate your success as a freelancer. For many—possibly most—people, money will be the critical determinant. But how do you know if your freelance business really is financially rewarding? Measure your current freelance income against three criteria:

Your business plan. Does your income match the objectives you set or reset (see Tip 12)? If so, give yourself credit for achieving your goals on schedule. You have a right to be optimistic. If your income greatly exceeds your goals, determine whether your business plan was too modest—or you've simply created a success beyond anything you'd expected. Either way, you're in great shape. Is your income lower than planned? Review your annual report (see Tip 39) and revised business plan to determine whether you understand the reasons for your shortfall and whether the actions you plan to take stand a reasonable chance of bringing you closer to your objectives.

Employee compensation. Based on your experience as an employee, information you gather from people in your industry, and published surveys of salaries, measure how you stack up against people doing the same job but working for others. If you're making more money than you would expect to earn as an employee, you're doing well. If not, don't give up freelancing yet, because you also have to weigh your income against . . .

Long-term trends. During my first full year of freelancing I netted only about 55 percent of what I would have made as an employee. Had I used that year's metric alone as a yardstick, I would eagerly have sought shelter with an employer. And that would have been a terrible mistake. Business growth, and a corresponding increase in income, takes time. My second-year income topped that of the first year by 55 percent. I knew that comparable growth the following year would push my income above what I would have been making as an employee. That growth took two years, but it happened. By doing the math and charting your trends, you'll be able to see the point at which freelancing becomes financially advantageous.

Avoid a rush to judgment in your first years. I experienced no growth in my third year, then phenomenal growth thereafter to quickly reach and pass the $100,000 mark. Measure your financial achievements carefully and over time, and you may achieve more than you ever thought possible.

TIP 99

Enter analysis.

Think beyond income to decide whether freelancing offers you other rewards that include control, time, and contentment.

I've always remembered the advice my mother, Blanche, gave me when I was still in college. "I don't care what you do," she said.

"Just do it well." My mother never mentioned money except in the most general terms: "Make a living for your family." Both my parents left it to me to decide what that living might be. (Of course, she did advise me, "It's as easy to fall in love with a rich girl as a poor one.") Once I graduated from college, I was on my own to earn the best living I could in whatever way I could.

It was not money, however, that drove me into freelancing. Unhappy with my job, lacking the time to find a better one, and wanting to spend more time with my firstborn, Seth, I saw a number of other rewards in working for myself and never dreamed of setting a $100,000 income as a goal.

If you're a freelancer wondering about packing it in or an employee investigating the possibilities of working solo, you can't help thinking about money. But analyze what really makes you happy and give consideration to several other contingencies that often outweigh dollars alone.

Control. Being your own boss involves taking on new and challenging responsibilities. But being responsible for your own well-being can be invigorating. You have the freedom to choose the projects you want to work on, deal with clients you like and reject those you don't, and harvest all the rewards of your effort rather than yield them to your boss or corporate headquarters.

Flexibility. The nineties ushered a measure of flexibility into the workplace, but most employees still realize that as long as they work for someone else, they work by someone else's rules. You come to work when the company tells you to come to work. You telecommute when the company says you can telecommute. You stay late when the company wants you to stay late. You vacation when the company schedule allows you to vacation. Admittedly, freelancing is not necessarily a day at the beach. Unless you have an independent income, you have to work to succeed. But you also have the option of trading dollars for time—to sleep late on Fridays, jog during lunchtime, shop in the afternoon and work after dinner, take your children to nursery school and pick them up for playtime *before* dinner. You might surrender some income to do it, but *you* make the choices.

Contentment. For many employees, career and burnout are synonymous. Long hours and separation from family create stress. Office politics creates more stress. And millions of Americans struggle through the commute from hell twice a day because it's impossible to find affordable housing close to work. Even higher salaries cease to become an incentive when you analyze the cost of gasoline, insurance, wear and tear on your car, day care and babysitter fees, and doctor and pharmacy bills related to stress-induced physical and emotional illnesses. Add an ongoing feeling of fatigue incongruously matched with sleepless nights and weekends that disappear in nanoseconds, and the value of a dollar becomes open to discussion. Freelancing can be demanding, but it offers you the opportunity to adjust your lifestyle to your income, slow your pace, and seek rewards that money truly cannot provide.

What's most important to you? Find a quiet time and place, and *write down* what you like about being an employee and what you don't. List the things you like about your life and those you don't. And determine the real financial costs of being an employee as well as the salary and benefits.

Discover what really makes you happy, and you'll discover the right path to take—whichever path that may be.

TIP 100

Keep it personal.

Do business ethically to preserve your good name, stay productive each day, and sleep peacefully every night.

In scene after scene of Francis Ford Coppola's Oscar-winning *Godfather* trilogy, a gangster who is about to kill, has killed, or has attempted to kill another, repeats some version of a wickedly revealing refrain: "It's nothing personal. Only business." Several times, mafiosi comment about how much they respect or like their victims. Murder is simply another part of "a day at the office," and they want to make clear that neither the victims nor their families should let their feelings be hurt or confused by violent death.

The more I think about this attitude, the more chilling it becomes. For the crime families in *The Godfather*, life is merely a commodity. If someone poses an obstacle to a deal—as Don Corleone stands in the way of a younger man's proposed drug enterprise—remove the obstacle. It's only business.

As billionaire investor-philanthropist George Soros wrote in the *Atlantic Monthly*, "The cult of success has replaced a belief in principles. Society has lost its anchor."

I would be remiss if I didn't conclude with this last tip, because no matter what the nature of your freelance business, it *is* personal. Anyone in contact with the corporate world has gone through the "business is war" analogy more than once. I remember editing the introductory speeches to a company's sales meeting that featured a military theme, officers' titles for the senior executives, and endless military metaphors. Once you get involved with that kind of thinking, it's easy to take the next step toward "It's only business."

Regrettably, too many individuals—from Fortune 500 CEOs to freelancers—believe that success can be achieved only by casting aside the rules and ethics we have been taught to live by. Hillel taught us not to do to others what we wouldn't want to have done to ourselves. Jesus approached this teaching from another angle and taught us to do unto others what we would have them do to us. Yet the business world abounds with people who rationalize the importance of "doing unto others *before* they do unto you." They make the world a sadder place.

Keep it personal, and you'll enjoy several important advantages that money cannot buy:

A good name. Never scoff at the importance of reputation. It's a freelancer's biggest asset. From adding new clients to maintaining the relationships you've worked so hard to develop, your success will ultimately depend on what others think of your integrity. Jeopardize your good name once, and word will spread faster than an oil slick in a choppy sea. Trust really is the foundation on which business success is built.

A good day at the office. It's no accident that death or violent disappointment strikes every key member of the Corleone family. They have doomed themselves. The don has to bear Sonny's death in an ambush and Michael's entry into the business rather than into politics, as he had planned. Rivals kill Michael's first wife in an attempt on his life. His second wife divorces him. Michael has his brother Fredo killed right after their mother dies. In turn, new rivals in Sicily kill Michael's daughter in a botched assassination attempt at the conclusion of *The Godfather Part III*. What goes around . . .

A good night's sleep. Hamlet decries the fact that "Conscience doth make cowards of us all." That's not the half of it. Conscience also produces insomniacs by the millions. My father, Morris, was probably the most ethical person I've ever known. To his family, friends, coworkers, and customers, his name was synonymous with honesty and integrity. Not inconsequentially, when he laid his head on his pillow at night, he slept undisturbed by anything he had done or failed to do that day. Inner peace has no price.

Struggle and strive to meet your goals as a freelancer, whatever they may be. As long as you remember that business is very personal, your freelance business will bring you personal satisfaction year after year.

A LITTLE EXTRA ADVICE

Now that you've read *Solo Success*, you're ready to put these 100 proven tips to work. But just as doughnut shop and bagel bakery clerks place something extra in your bag to make a baker's dozen, let me include a little extra advice given to me over the years. Without question, it has helped me through my difficult periods. Apply these extra tips to your freelance business, and the 100 tips you've just read will become even more valuable. Make them part of your life, and I really believe that you'll find yourself more contented regardless of what transpires with your business.

"Never lose your sense of humor"—Dr. Melvin Bernstein, professor of English, Alfred University. Maybe my college years were grimmer than I thought, but I've treasured Doc's advice for decades. When things are not going well—and even the most successful freelancers have tough weeks and months—seeing the funny side of a situation can keep you on an even keel.

"When it's getting too hot for you, it's just getting right for me"—Staff Sergeant Thomas "Fat Cat" Johnson, U.S. Army Basic Training Center, Fort Dix, New Jersey. The Fat Cat didn't go to college, but he knew a lot more than many of the college graduates who sweated under his tutelage. Thanks to a warm sense of humor, he had the rare ability to push our platoon and make us want to extend ourselves at the same time. Of course, he wasn't crawling through sand or going through bayonet drills in ninety-five-degree weather. Then again, he'd earned his Combat Infantryman's Badge in Korea. But no one communicated Kipling's advice of keeping your head when those about you are losing theirs better than he did. I still hear his voice when stress begins to build.

"Always be a professional"—Dr. Louis Schuster, professor of English, Saint Mary's University, San Antonio. I studied with this Chaucer scholar when I worked on my M.A. at night on the G.I. Bill while working at an ad agency during the day. Being a member of a religious order didn't separate Brother Louis from everyday reality. Simply put, performing a task under adverse circumstances separates those who do from those who don't. The pros advance. Everyone else falls behind.

"Do it now"—Morris Perlstein. Above all, I was fortunate to have had an example set for me by my father. A salesman for a large manufacturer of springs for the furniture and bedding industry, he built his own considerable success by working as if the company were his own. Because of the nature of sales, he had to carefully manage his time as well as his relationships with his customers. As a result, he immediately did whatever had to be done. Like most teenagers and young men, I generally fell to procrastinating. As I matured, his words guided me well. Today I frequently ask myself, "What would Dad do?" Then I do it. Right away.

At this point you're more than prepared to take on the challenges of freelancing and earn the rewards commensurate with your efforts. Keep your business in perspective, and you'll keep your life in perspective. Good luck!

INDEX